PRAISE FOR
MIKE DOOLEY

"These are the best emails I ever receive and are a spark for me at this time on this journey. Mike, this is a wonderful form of service that has chosen YOU."

"Thank you ever so much for your Monday Morning Motivators. If you only knew how much I enjoy them. Every Monday I find myself gasping with disbelief ... somehow each Monday your motivators relate to every situation that is currently going on in my life. What a wonderful gift you give to me each Monday! Please continue to send them on."

"When I first read [your emails] I cried.
It is just so incredible to me to know that there are people out there, who I don't know (on a physical level anyway) that GET IT!"

"I have been receiving your inspirational quotes and words for some time now ... You are really making a difference."

"You can never know how much your latest email meant to me. I am in the most transitional period of my life here on earth and your message was a gift. Thank you."

"Just wanted you to know how much I enjoy the emails. The words you speak are filled with TRUTH. The past few years of my life have been quite an eye opening experience as I realize more and more every day the unlimited potential that everyone possesses. Just having that knowledge is AWESOME! Keep the good vibes a-flowing!"

"I've been getting the Monday Motivator some time now. They're simply great. Of course I create my own reality, and of course my mission on earth is to be happy and love…but it's so easy to forget and your messages are so clear and a great reminder to use during my day. Keep it up. Thanks for your part in contributing to the enlightenment of the planet."

"Thank you for the positive energy you bring to my life."

"I really do LOVE getting your emails they are so uplifting and when I have bad days, these seem to pull me through."

"This is fantastic! You are right on the money with where I am spiritually at this time in my life! There are no accidents!"

"I cannot believe how many times you touch my life every week in a way that no one reaches. It is almost like you are reading my thoughts, my prayers, and wishes. Thank you for the uplifts, they are greatly needed and appreciated!"

"You had no way of knowing, of course, but your messages of encouragement and calls to action have helped to get me through a very difficult year. Thanks!"

"Thank you for the wonderful words, thoughts, and inspiration. I appreciate every morsel."

"This is amazing … the way you think, the way these messages come to me when I need them most. My life is so negative lately, and your messages are the ones that prod me along, telling me to keep going and search for the happiness again. It's the next best thing to having someone so encouraging by my side."

"I just have to tell you, that I love what you send me every Monday! I also get other inspirational/motivational pieces, but none of them compare to what you share with me."

"Your thoughts are poetic and greatly cherished. You are a special individual with a wondrous perspective on life. I see the world through 'rose-colored glasses' and it's nice to know that others do too."

"Thanks so much for reminding me that peace, contentment, and joy are already mine."

"You are an eloquent master of weaving words not only into pictures, but into feelings of radiant joy and love. It is a joy to see someone in their bliss"

"May God be with you always as you continue to touch our lives. Thank you for sharing your thoughts, for keeping us company in our solitude, for giving hope in times of trouble, and for simply being a friend to all of us."

Choose Them Wisely

Also by Mike Dooley

Notes from the Universe

More Notes from the Universe

Even More Notes from the Universe

Infinite Possibilities

Coming in November 2010

Manifesting Change

Choose Them Wisely

Thoughts Become Things!

MIKE DOOLEY

ATRIA PAPERBACK
New York London Toronto Sydney

BEYOND WORDS
Hillsboro, Oregon

ATRIA PAPERBACK
A Division of Simon & Schuster, Inc.
1230 Avenue of the Americas
New York, NY 10020

BEYOND WORDS
20827 N.W. Cornell Road, Suite 500
Hillsboro, Oregon 97124-9808
503-531-8700 / 503-531-8773 fax
www.beyondword.com

Managing editor: Lindsay S. Brown
Editor: Marie Hix
Copyeditor: Marvin Moore
Proofreader: Gretchen Stelter
Design: Devon Smith

First Atria Books/Beyond Words trade paperback edition June 2010

ATRIA PAPERBACK and colophon are trademarks of Simon & Schuster, Inc. Beyond Words Publishing is a division of Simon & Schuster, Inc.

For more information about special discounts for bulk purchases, please contact Simon & Schuster Special Sales at 1-800-506-1949 or business@simonandschuster.com.

The Simon & Schuster Speakers Bureau can bring authors to your live event. For more information or to book an event contact the Simon & Schuster Speakers Bureau at 1-866-248-3049 or visit our website at www.simonspeakers.com.

Manufactured in the United States of America

10 9 8 7 6 5 4 3

Library of Congress Cataloging-in-Publication Data

Dooley, Mike.
   Choose them wisely : thoughts become things! / Mike Dooley.
     p. cm.
   1. New Thought--Miscellanea. I. Title.
   BF639.D66 2009
   158--dc22
                              2008044307

ISBN 978-1-58270-225-4 (hc)
ISBN 978-1-58270-233-9 (pbk)
ISBN 978-1-4391-0987-8 (ebook)

The corporate mission of Beyond Words Publishing, Inc.: Inspire to Integrity

To Calli and Sarah

Unlimited, mysterious,
powerful, sublime—
the least that you are
in space and time.

CONTENTS

contents

Contents

Contents

Contents

Contents

Contents

contents

Contents

PREFACE

In the late 1990s, shortly after the birth of the internet, the little company Mom, Andy, and I had started in 1989, "Totally Unique T-shirts," or TUT, began collecting email addresses from visitors to our retail stores. Shortly thereafter, I sent out my first "Monday Morning Motivator" to thirty-six people. They were simply inspirational poems taken from our bestselling T-shirts. I never added any commentary to those first mailings; I just followed the poem with mention of any retail specials we were having.

In 1999, with T-shirt sales and our own enthusiasm declining, we decided to liquidate our business while we were still ahead financially, regroup, and reinvent ourselves. By the time this was accomplished, all that remained of our family business that had sold over one million T-shirts was its domain name (www.tut.com) and a database of about 1,500 email addresses. Not wanting to let these go and

feeling that the internet could prove to be a salvation yet, I continued sending out the Monday missives, but instead of following each poem with a "deal of the week," I mustered the courage to add a paragraph or two of insight, expounding on the message and lesson of the poem—and vo-o-o-o-o-m! The response was instantaneous.

Suddenly, I received confirmation from the voids of cyberspace that my weekly emails were actually reaching human beings, because for the first time in years of sending them, people began to reply with notes of their own, which usually went something like this: "Wow! I hope you're saving these for a book one day!" "You have no idea how much your thoughts this morning meant to me." "I'm looking forward to Mondays because of you!" Of course, as a free service that wasn't offering anything for sale, this was entirely a "nonprofit" venture, but I felt certain that I was on to something.

So, in between updating my résumé and responding to

employment ads all over the country, I devoted more and more time to my weekly mailings and the website that would support them, writing about the truths that I most needed to embrace in order to change my own life. And just as it became apparent how small the demand was for an executive who had just liquidated his own company, TUT's Adventurers Club began sprouting wings. "A philosophical club for the adventure of life," its weekly emails soon became daily emails—which finally evolved into the now wildly popular *Notes from the Universe*, with over 270,000 subscribers and growing. At times, I can hardly believe the swift reversal and rise of my good fortunes. My "nonprofit" venture has become fantastically successful, evolving into audio programs, an appearance in *The Secret*, book deals, worldwide speaking engagements, and a nonprofit charity organization called Gifts from the Universe.

Even for me, it's almost hard to believe that this turn of events wasn't somehow meant to be, but I know better. I remember all too well the forks that lay in the road just

eight years ago and how "career" certainty and monetary gains were virtually nonexistent, tempting me to run for safety down paths that promised little else. But as I now tell my readers, if you understand the nature of reality, that our thoughts unfailingly become the things and events of our lives, and you let go of the past and all the labels you have accumulated while "thinking what you know to think, saying what you know to say, and doing what you know to do," it will always be enough.

Until now, the original "Monday Morning Motivators" that started everything have been collecting dust in a three-ring binder. But as a reader once enthusiastically suggested, I have, indeed, saved them for a book—and this is it.

Tallyho,

How You Might Use This Book

When these messages were first sent out by email to subscribers, the most common reply I received—and still receive to this day—was that more often than not, day after day, readers were amazed by the uncanny timing of each one as it related to exactly where they were in their respective lives: "Thank you VERY much for the sentiment you sent today. By some miracle it was EXACTLY what I needed! I printed it out and posted it on my bulletin board to read, hourly if need be!" or "You had no way of knowing, of course, but your messages of encouragement and calls to action have helped to get me through a very difficult year. Thanks."

Though thousands of people will read these messages, each person will filter them through their own thoughts, history, and circumstances. Plus, in the jungles of time and space, things are not as they appear. We've been told since our lives began that we are but mere bystanders to the glory of life and

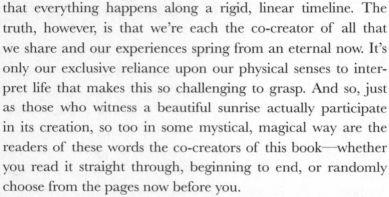

that everything happens along a rigid, linear timeline. The truth, however, is that we're each the co-creator of all that we share and our experiences spring from an eternal now. It's only our exclusive reliance upon our physical senses to interpret life that makes this so challenging to grasp. And so, just as those who witness a beautiful sunrise actually participate in its creation, so too in some mystical, magical way are the readers of these words the co-creators of this book—whether you read it straight through, beginning to end, or randomly choose from the pages now before you.

Go on, give it a try. Just open this book to any "random" page and see what you get. You're really quite the writer, you know.

What once was a dream
has now come to pass,
as the stone and the clay
were first ether and gas.

GOT GLUE?

Talk a little, sing a lot,
walk a little, dance a lot,
smile a little, laugh a lot,
dream a little, live a lot.††

Living the life of your dreams isn't just about dreaming; it's also about living—following your impulses, turning over every stone, and stepping out into the world so that the wind can catch your sails.

See, it's as if your dreams paint the picture and the Universe stands ready to bring it to life. You just have to go outside and move around in the proper directions so that the old picture and the new can be seamlessly fused together.

Every single door you open this week, every hand you shake, and every smile you flash will actually give the Universe another front, another chance, to slip into your life with its magic and wonders, to cut and paste, and fuse on.

Live a lot!

WARNING!!
THOUGHTS BECOME THINGS!

Choose them wisely.

Not just sometimes but all of the time. And not just your good thoughts but the other ones too! It's an immutable law, as rigid and predictable as gravity. In fact, you can't ever turn it off. But, of course, this isn't bad news; it's awesome news, because they're your thoughts and every minute of every day you get to choose exactly what you'll think!

What a great way to run a reality. Could it be any easier than getting what you think about? And never will it be a game about moving around the props but rather of moving around the images in our minds.

Our physical bodies, our dramas, and the props on the stage are just mirrored reflections of our beliefs and expectations about each. Change the thoughts and the Universe changes the props, be they people, places, or things.

You don't have to work more hours, get more schooling, shake more hands, climb more ladders, or make more sacrifices. You just have to weave the dream!

ME, ME, ME!

Since the dawn of time
we've been one and the same.
Your smile and laughter
have been my sole aim.
I am the voice you hear
when the sky turns gray
and the hand you hold
when you've lost your way.
So never forget,
when the chips are down,
I'm busy at work
to turn things around.

A long, long time ago, you and your celestial family were checking out the brochures of time and space, and being the adventurous one among them, you shrieked, "Me, me, me! I want to go! I want to live as a creation amongst my creations in a paradise cloaked in matter, with dominion over all things!"

And your family's infinitely wise and compassionate patriarch thought about it, and thought about it, and thought about it. And finally your patriarch said, "Loved one, you do realize that there are certain challenges that go along with living in time and space? Huge challenges. First off, there's the amnesia. Then, there's the illusion of being separate from everything and everyone. Feelings of loss and fear are rampant. And just when you think it's safe to go out, there's bad hair."

So you thought and you thought and you thought. And you finally asked, "Will things ever be as bad as they seem?"

"Never."

"Any chance I won't make it back? You know, here, where I'm everywhere at once, connected, loved, and adored, happy and free forever?"

"None."

"Will there be help and guidance?"

"Always."

"And you?"

"I'll never leave your side."

THINK BIG

Whatever you want ... wants you.

Imagine that there's another world, beyond the reach of your physical senses, just outside of time and space; a world that mirrors your own—not the physical things, but the intangibles; a world that mirrors your thoughts and dreams, your beliefs and expectations. And imagine that every thought you entertain comes to life in this other realm with a single mission: to "jump worlds" and join you in time and space.

Now, imagine that these two worlds run exactly parallel to one another and that they're invisibly fused together in the here and now.

Pretend that every here and now comes from this other world, from all your prior thoughts, not from your past, not from the world of time and space that surrounds you.

Do you realize what this would mean? It would mean that your future, beginning today, will not unfold based on your past or based upon the existing conditions of your life, but will unfold based entirely upon your thoughts and dreams, your beliefs and expectations.

OK, you can stop pretending and imagining because this is exactly how things really are. This is why all things are possible! All things come from thought, and your thoughts are determined by you.

How cool is that?

JUST CHECKING

"If you want to make God laugh
tell Her your plans
for the rest of your life?"

Not likely.

On the other hand, "If you want to make God, the Universe, and all of the angels bust up into absolute hysterics, tell 'em HOW your dreams will come true."

God, or the Universe, wants for you what you want for you. Yet from where you now stand, there's no way you can possibly see all that She sees or know all that She knows with regard to the infinite ways your dreams might come true the fastest.

Save yourself the trouble, the laughs, and from spinning your wheels, and simply never mess with the cursed HOWs.

HOW TO SAVE THE WORLD

You yearn,
you go.
You learn,
you grow.

You simply cannot give to the world all that you have to give to the world if you do not remain true to your own "selfish" desires. You have a unique set of precious values that can only be fulfilled by pursuing what drives you the most: your passions and dreams. Could Thomas Edison have tended to the downtrodden as Mother Teresa did? Could Albert Einstein have preached salvation as Martin Luther King Jr. did? Could Abraham Lincoln have built cars like Henry Ford? Always, the masses benefit from the individuals who insist on marching to the beat of their own drummer.

After all, if you don't follow your desires, then whose?

Your dreams and desires are of supreme importance, and they're yours for a reason—gifts from your higher self to remind you of what is possible.

Don't ignore them, hedge them, or fear them. And never, ever compromise them. Selfish? Well, if you don't safeguard your own happiness, you'll never be able to help others find theirs.

Be the example. Push, reach, and stretch-h-h-h. Attain, gloat, and revel. And during the journey, your light will shine on all our paths while revealing the truths you came here to know.

Hup, 2, 3, 4 ...

ROSE-COLORED GLASSES

See it all as easy,
And so it must become.

You don't need more books, more classes, more learning, or more intellect.

You have all you need to have all you want. Don't try to be different or smarter than you already are. The answers you seek lie in the present moment, and by enjoying whatever it is that you enjoy and by following your heart out into the world—no matter what others might think—your questions will be answered, your step will be made lighter, and you will see how true this is and how easy life has always been.

Besides, rose is such a great color on you.

USE IT OR LOSE IT

When you think
a brand new thought,
something comes alive.
And when you think
this brand new thought,
it will strive and strive and strive
to find its place
in time and space,
to reach the light of day.
So think your new thought all the time
to help it find its way!

Definitely hokey, but thoughts really do become things. It's a law—an objective, uncaring law—like gravity or magnetism. These laws don't care if you deserve them. They don't care if you've been bad or good. They don't care if you know they exist. And they don't work better if you believe in them.

They just are. You can't change them, but you can use them.

You can let gravity wear you down, or you can use it to climb mountains. You can let magnetism lie latent, or you can harness it to power a nation. And you can choose to think idly and reactively, or you can craft a life based on your wildest dreams!

IT'S ME! LIFE!

Thoughts are the things
that draw life to you.
Like a magnet to steel,
they're how dreams come true.
It's really that easy
and a whole lot of fun,
just know what you want
and imagine it done.

Sure, the manifestation part is easy. You already do it, day in and day out. Your dreams have come true. You're living them right now! The heroes and heroines in your life—they're pretty much what you thought you'd find, right? And the hills and valleys, the challenges and triumphs are just like you pictured them. You've got the right stuff, and you're using it!

The tricky part, and this isn't always so obvious, is knowing what you really want. Tricky because it requires brutal honesty with yourself. It requires asking questions that ordinarily you wouldn't have to ask, looking at the facts you've "made up," rethinking what they're proving, and understanding your fears and your true motivations.

No, of course you don't have to go there. Almost no one does. You can fool most of the people most of the time, and no one's going to come tap you on the shoulder to tell you that you've been kidding yourself.

Accept the life you lead.

Question yourself and think deep.

YOU ARE PERFECT

A flower is simple,
its message is true:
The earth is happy,
there are people like you —
just as you are!

Wow, the pressure! To be all that you can be, to achieve all that you can achieve, and to help all that you can help! But here's the truth: You can't possibly be any more than you now are. You are perfect; "it" is done; the plan is unfolding.

Nothing you think, nothing you will ever achieve—no ribbons, medals, dollars, or "thank yous"—will ever compare to the significance of your being just who you are. You don't have to do anything else. Your presence in time and space is enough. You are the Universe seeing itself; you are the invisible expressing as the visible. Your eyes see things that no others will ever see,

and your ears hear things that only you can hear, and so it is that all that you are is rare and special and precious. Your view of reality is invariably shared with all that is. And without you, all that is would be less.

You can't outdo you, so lighten up with all the "to dos," the "shoulds," and the "musts," and appreciate the magnificence that you already are. No wonder there are so many flowers.

BE THE SPARK

Action begets action;
Yours begets mine.

You know that feeling when all of a sudden it seems like everything you ever wanted to happen starts happening at once? When you're totally blown away, on top of the world, almost feeling like you don't even have any more dreams because they're all coming true?

Yet, you're slammed because you're stretching yourself like you've never stretched before, just trying to keep up with your dreams, and everyday some new magical realization hits you. And you've never felt so happy in your life, except that you wish so badly that everyone close to you could have the same over-whelming experiences, the same sensory overload; and more, you wish everyone on the planet could feel it too, at least just a little, because it's so intoxicating.

Now, you feel like you understand all the tough times, all the slow days, and all the phases when it seemed like absolutely nothing was happening in your life, and you wonder why you haven't always felt like this, because what you feel is so much more than just the joy of dreams coming true; it's like you're feeling the heartbeat of everyone's life at once.

You begin to realize that there's always been so much more to be happy about than sad, and you wonder what it was that used to trouble you and how it could have seemed so real or how it could've seemed bigger than the beauty you now face.

You just shake your head, knowing how perfect everything is, how perfect it's always been, and how perfect it will always be, and you give thanks, with your hands over face, tasting the salt of your tears, because you know that this, this feeling, more than anything else you've ever experienced, was so meant to be.

IMAGINATION

Imagination ... is everything!

Imagination establishes the blueprint for what can happen within time and space. Without the blueprint there is no image, pattern, or mold for reality to follow. Imagination gives the Universe direction. It's the steering wheel or rudder on the ship of your dreams. And this isn't true sometimes; it's true all the time. Thoughts become things, no matter what you're thinking. So think the good ones!

And sometimes it all seems so real, doesn't it? Next time the mud hits the fan, remember that your real challenge begins with using your imagination, not combating or manipulating a physical world that only mirrors what you used to think about.

You are here to learn of your power, your divinity, and your sovereignty, not to be batted about by illusions, lost in a sea of mystery, or suffering for sins you don't even remember committing—or even the ones you do remember. There is no other agenda.

Think the good thoughts and your life will be transformed. It's the law!

OWN IT

If you see it, touch it.
If you touch it, feel it.
If you feel it, love it.
And when you love it, give it,
and more will be added
unto you.

B ecause nothing speaks to the Universe louder of your belief in self, abundance, and love than giving.

And when the Universe hears, more will be added to you. Not as a reward but because you truly believed in self, abundance, and love.

Yee-ha! What a way to run the world! And best of all, this is your world! Think of the possibilities. They're endless! Notice that there are no references above to blood, sweat, and tears. No implications of sacrifice, commitment, or years. Not a hint of judgment, luck, or coincidences. Nary an exception!

You're not here to experience lack, disease, or impediments. You're here to experience dominion over all things. So go, own, and know. But be careful because this chain reaction is a lot harder to stop than it is to start.

PLENTY OF TIME

"Where" you are is never "who" you are.
You're always more.
Infinitely more.

Being spiritual means a good many things, but a good many people misunderstand most of them. So to clarify, here's how I see it and you: Being spiritual means seeing yourself as divine, not just of the divine— a creator, not just the created. You needn't be saved, forgiven, or fixed. You've already changed the world, added to its brilliance, and done enough. You're there because, in some long forgotten time, you already earned your wings.

Of course, there are still challenges. You wanted it this way; it's part of your nature and these challenges will serve to make you even greater. In spite of these, you are still a winner; you are among the relative few who have been so bold, and today is part of your victory lap.

HOW TO MAKE HISTORY!

Dream on and dream big:
they're all meant to be.
Just imagine them done
and they're history.

Never, ever underestimate the power of your imagination! Your thoughts literally reach out from you to the farthest corners of the earth. They tap every living soul on the shoulder. They mingle with the "gods." And finally, they return to you as the material things and events of your life. They really do!

Are you lonely? Are you bored? Are you frightened? Are you embattled? Are you stressed? Are you ill? Are you living with less than abundance? There is no job that can't be tackled by thought.

Here's the trick: Focus your thinking on what you want, not on what you have. Think of where you're going, not of where you are. Then give thanks that it's already done and follow your impulses. It's that easy!

Thoughts, your thoughts, are what engage the invisible principles that operate all things in time and space—principles that are absolute, inviolate, and unmovable; principles that every prophet or messiah who has ever graced the face of the earth has tried to tell us about; principles that do not pass judgment; principles that just deliver, as they have all your life.

What you think will make a difference, thank heavens!

AREN'T YOUNG SOULS CUTE?

Young souls look to secrets, rights, and rituals.
Advanced souls look to science, math, and evidence.
And old souls... old souls look within.

Anyhow, the one thing I know for sure is that with time, and by looking within, everything becomes clear, all questions are answered, what's broken is restored, new trails are blazed, hearts are mended, love returns, and you will look over your shoulder at life's utter perfection with a tear in your eye.

And best of all, time is one thing we souls have plenty of.

VISUALIZE YOUR HAPPINESS

Every thought you think sends waves into motion.
Every word you speak reaches millions of ears.
And every act you perform literally rearranges the stars.
Now, what was it you wanted me to do for you?

In a world as totally awesome as yours, where do you even start?

Visualize. Just once a day, because if you do it more, you may become too anxious over the future you are dreaming of, perhaps becoming discouraged. Besides, why do it more when there is so much you already have and so much you already are that can be enjoyed in the present?

Visualize the ultimate emotion you're after: happiness. Feel the joy. Hear yourself excitedly talking and laughing with friends.

Emotion, after all, is what supercharges your thoughts and accelerates the manifestation of your dreams. Practice FEELING what you really want to feel. Not only will you draw experiences that will match those feelings into your life, but you will achieve it all so much faster!

OH YEAH

A life is not measured
by the games that are won,
but that you lived in the moment
and learned how to have fun.

Remember that feeling of being invincible, optimistic, wide-eyed, and carefree? Remember that excited sense of anticipation you have felt for most of your life? Remember plotting your course around "the fun" and saying, "Let's get together" often? When almost every day was an adventure?

Oh no, uh-uh, don't go there!

First of all, back then, you never even knew you felt like that. It's only with the clarity of hindsight that you can now see the magic that really did hold you in the palm of its hand. And today, you are still carried, ever so lovingly, by that very same magic. Choose to feel it again, now. It never left you. It's still there. Don't let another year or ten or more go by before you recognize today's magic. Because right here and now, even

more so than back then, you are poised to have more fun than you have ever had before.

Oh yeah!

"Let's get together."

Having fun is why you're here. It's not frivolous; it's not just for kids; it's important! And the art of having fun lies in appreciating wherever you are, whenever you are. Its potential hides at work; it hides in your routines; it even lurks in bumper-to-bumper traffic! It begins by realizing that every moment that ticks by brings you closer to manifesting your heart's desires, understanding life's mysteries, and comprehending that you are bathed in love always. It is a wonderful life and it offers endless opportunities for fun to those who seek even when they wouldn't think of seeking!

Here's hoping you find plenty this week!

THE ADVENTURERS CLUB OATH

It's time to renew our vows,
while not worrying about the hows...

In the face of adversity, uncertainty, and conflicting sensory information, I hereby pledge to remain ever mindful of the magical, infinite, loving reality I live in— a reality that conspires tirelessly in my favor. I further recognize that living within space and time, as a creation amongst my creations, is the ultimate adventure because thoughts become things, dreams do come true, and all things remain forever possible. As a Being of Light, I hereby resolve to live, love, and be happy at all costs, no matter what, with reverence and kindness for all. So be it!

Your wishes are what the Universe wishes for you, and your thoughts actually steer the ship of your dreams. This is the truth! And no matter where you've been or how challenging your circumstances, right here and now is all that matters, because you are forever invincible—a Being of Light on an adventure of the highest order: to have fun and be happy.

You are powerful beyond measure.

THE EQUATION OF
REALITY CREATION

Every day you move mountains, touch lives, and perform miracles.
Every day you're a success, a hero, an example.
And every day you change the world.

By the simple act of thinking, vortexes are created, invisible energies are applied, and circumstances begin creeping to make real what was previously just imagined. This supernatural pull of your thoughts continues long after you think them, whenever intent, expectation, and action follow, moving mountains, parting rivers, and doing the "impossible" until there is the inevitable manifestation.

This is how your "thoughts become things," how they physically become things in a dimension that already exists, with billions of players and massive momentum. Not by appearing out of thin air, but through a manipulation of such forces in the unseen that literally begin shifting, morphing, and arranging all of the elements in your life so as to deliver to you the nearest equivalent of what you've been thinking. In other words, the law of attraction.

"Thoughts becoming things" explains the law of attraction. It's why there is a law of attraction. And unlike any other three words in all the vocabularies of all the languages in the world, "thoughts become things" tells you exactly where you fit into the picture, as the thinker, the decision maker over what you will think about, revealing your power as a supernatural, all powerful, unlimited CREATOR.

But, of course, many prefer not to think of themselves as so phenomenally powerful.

I'm glad you're different. You're going to change things quite a bit... Whoa!

INFINITE YOU

An infinite drop
in an infinite sea,
like an infinite you
and an infinite me.

We are unlimited, living in a reality that possesses seemingly magical powers which obey our every command. What has been done by one can be done by all. And all "doing" is done by simply thinking of what it is you want to do and having the conviction to physically move with those thoughts.

Moving with your thoughts, "acting as if," tells the Universe you believe in what you've dreamed, allowing and even accelerating the dream's entry into the time and space of your immediate life. You do this already. It's how you do all things. It's even how you create limits—thinking of them and

moving accordingly! Just become aware of the process to understand and master your infinite self.

It's the invisible things you think that really make things rock and roll! For a one-two punch that will move mountains, follow your invisible thoughts with little daily actions—preparatory acts of faith that are aligned with your new thinking. Then get out of the way!

IMAGINATION RULES

It's really quite simple;
you just have to believe
that life is for living
the dreams you conceive.

Nothing on earth is more powerful than your thoughts—nothing. Nothing can make you happier, healthier, wealthier, and wiser, nor sadder, sicker, poorer, or dumber! They travel faster than light. They reach the ends of the earth and touch every person in between. They trump all physical laws. They're free. They come to you effortlessly. And you get to choose your favorite ones.

Yet for all their power, there is a reason why your thoughts might not serve your highest and best interests, and it's frightfully prevalent. It's actually rampant, even contagious. It's this: People, even people who understand the above points—especially people who understand the above points—mistakenly think that knowing this stuff is the same as living this stuff. It's not.

Today and this week, may you begin living this stuff; harnessing your thoughts; willfully choosing them; dwelling on the abundance, health, and harmony that the Universe is now pushing out to you; visualizing; acting "as if;" and giving thanks that your dreams have already come true. It's worth it! Your dreams are worth it! You're worth it! And it's easy!

Believe in your inevitable success because it is inevitable. You can't lose as an unlimited Being of Light who lives in a world where imagination rules, where thoughts become things and all things are possible. You are eternal, forever, and unending. Nothing can change this, and as sure as there will be a tomorrow, you will inevitably triumph in the happiest of ways.

THE GREAT SLIDE

Start it; you don't have to be fancy.
Keep moving; you don't have to go crazy.
Visualize; you don't have to admit it.
See the end result; it doesn't have to be material.
Expect miracles; they don't have to be huge.
Pretend you've arrived; you don't have to dance on tables.
And above all else, have fun.
This is why you started it, right?

Once upon a time, there was a far, far away planet, and for one very long night that seemed to last for many thousands of years, it kept a great and epic secret. During this time, it was a place where even angels feared to tread. Its sun was afraid to rise. And its moon never really knew whether it was full or not.

And on this long night, rumors ran wild, tales grew tall, and without our even knowing it, the "Great Slide" began. I know, of course, because I was there. And while I don't like to admit it, that night nearly scared the pants off me.

That night, the first modern Halloween ever, you dressed up "human."

What started out as a game, something light and playful, like pin the halo on an angel, turned into a legacy that has haunted many a soul. You see, believe it or not, the more seriously we take ourselves, the more limited we become.

As that spooky night unfolded and gave way to eons, chaos gained momentum. Folks became frightened of their own manifestations, reacting to them instead of recreating them. In tangling with the cursed "hows," wishing took the place of deciding, dreams were dashed by hoping instead of knowing, and prayers began ending in question marks. Worst of all, as most became weaker and weaker, they resorted to visualizing what they wanted without knocking on doors, yearning without expecting, and, you guessed it, just kind of hanging around waiting for Oprah to call instead of living a life worth calling about.

Yeah, you know which planet I'm talking about. And yes, their secret that long and lonely night was that they were truly divine, capable of moving heaven and earth, and having it all, yet few would dare even whisper it for fear of being labeled "new agey."

WHY DO YOU "NEED"?

To want,
to need,
to dream,
and to grow
reveals the secrets
you came here to know.

Our desires come first; they lead us forward. Then later, as we find ourselves in the thick of things, "needs" crop up. We need to survive because we want to live. But which is more important? Which is less honorable? Desires are often thought of as selfish or frivolous, while needs are essential and natural. But considering their ordering, can needs be respected if desires are suppressed?

Both needs and desires are part of the curriculum here. And their gifts lie more in where they will take you than in their realization. Without either what would compel us to go forward, to achieve, to experience, and to be our totally unique selves?

Honor your passions as much as your needs—whatever they are. Look to understand the rewards they promise and enjoy the ride they inspire.

HERE AND NOW

Cast yesterday aside
and bid tomorrow adieu,
because there's nothing
here and now
that you can't do.

As supremely powerful as your thoughts of yesterday were, there's something else that can blow them all away, and those are your thoughts of today. Here and now is where and how.

Dwell on what could have been or what should have been and the disappointments of yesterday will revisit you today and be projected into your future. Hinge your happiness on tomorrow and it'll always lie a day away, like the carrot on a stick.

Your powers of appreciation and manifestation lie in the moment, this very moment, without regard to the past or the future. In fact, once you finish with this page, your chosen focus and attention will dictate how today will unfold.

Shazam!

37

THE MEANING OF ETERNITY

Each blossom forever blooms in its field;
each child forever clutches your hand;
each friend forever lingers in your heart.
This is what eternal means.

The truth is, you live in an infinitely kind and unspeakably wise Universe that you are a part of, not apart from—where you are a creator. And of your countless creations, your life is one. You chose to be here. And infinitely benign and intelligent, your choice was impeccable.

In this greatest adventure of all adventures, whatever you wish for sends legions into action on your behalf. The entire Universe is your most faithful servant and constant companion. Whatever you once dreamed of for yourself can still come to pass. It's never too late to come from behind, and things can

change for the better quite literally in the twinkling of an eye—
as you have so often demonstrated.

You are a supernatural being for whom all things are possible. And this, being a creation amongst your own creations, is as good as it gets, because whenever you don't like what's before you, you can change it. Without hindrance from the past or so-called contracts you no longer remember, thoughts become things; there are no other rules. There is no hidden agenda. And there are no unknown variables working against you in this Garden of Eden, this heaven on earth that we temporarily call home, where manifesting change most certainly couldn't be any easier than getting what you think about.

Oh yeah, way better than winning the lottery. Huh?

ETERNITY BEGINS TODAY

What has passed has passed
and matters no more.
Looking back in life
doesn't better the score.

What good could possibly come from dwelling on would have, could have, or should have?

Here and now is where it's at. Your decisions today are what matter. It's never too late. You're never too old. And eternity has just begun.

Let it be easy. No need to look back. The sun doesn't shine on days gone by.

Everything and everyone now in your life was put there by that great architect of your reality—you. Whatever you've brought into your life, you've brought for a reason. And whether or not that reason is obvious to you now, its objective will not

be met if you resist it. Face it, accept it, understand it, and move on. This doesn't mean you have to enjoy it nor do you have to keep it there, but pretending it doesn't exist just gives it extra staying power.

You're the great architect of your reality, right now as you read these very words. The plan has not been written; it's being written (present tense). Your bliss is now upon you; just write it into your plan. Expect it. Prepare for it. A celebration is near!

LOVE WHAT YOU DO

Do what you love,
love what you do,
and the world
will come to you! †

The first line of this "thought" is probably what makes the biggest impact. It's about believing in yourself and having the confidence to do what you want to do. Less striking, though just as powerful, is the second line. Loving what you do isn't about having the perfect job, the best home, or the smartest kids. And it's not about having a life without problems. In fact, it's not about having at all. It's about doing.

When you focus on what you do and not on what you have, you do it better, you have more fun, make a difference, touch more lives, and feel a sense of fulfillment that only doing can give you. The greatest irony, however, is that life becomes easier when you're having fun. The world becomes your oyster, including its many material goodies, which you well deserve!

This doesn't mean you have to learn to enjoy what you're doing. Things change, and so might what you decide to do from time to time. But it does mean that wherever you are today, you can start focusing on the doing and have fun making a difference in the lives that you touch.

JUST DO SOMETHING

The magic in life is far too great
to spend your time waiting on fate.
In just a blink, your dreams are born,
and when you act with faith,
they begin to take form.

Now, when it comes to your dreams, do you believe in them? Most people don't—not their big dreams—and so they don't prepare for them. But do you? Are you preparing? Well, to make sure you're on track, and to tip the scales in favor of their realization, start behaving as if their manifestation was absolutely inevitable. Because by acting with faith, even just once a day, you begin broadcasting to the Universe, as well as to yourself, that you do believe, and momentum is gathered.

Do things, little things, out of step with all the other things you do, that imply your dreams have and will come true.

Now don't just say, "Uh-huh. Yeah." Do something out of the ordinary—today! Something odd. Something you weren't going to do. Price shop a flight to New York or Nairobi for two—first class. Pick a date on your calendar to celebrate whatever it is you dream of celebrating. Practice signing your autograph and pick a standard salutation that you'll always use with it. Just do something. You'll see. It works.

Now, this will seem strange at first. Your mind will object. But that's how you'll know you're doing some good—more good than you could ever now grasp.

YOUR DESTINY

*A dream's just a dream
until you can see
yourself in the picture
like it was meant to be!*

Do you believe in fate? Ever feel that destiny plays a hand in your affairs? Like when everything in your life just "clicks" or when you meet a special person? If so, the following thought may come as a surprise: Absolutely nothing in the game of life is meant to be, except, of course, those things you most think about.

The only things that are truly meant to be are the things you deeply believe in—the things you expect to see in your life, which will generate the thoughts you constantly think, whether or not they're fun or painful.

You don't get the things you most want in life nor what providence has carved out for you, unless they're the things you think about the most—especially when you put yourself in the picture! The good news, the great news, is that you get to choose what you think! Seems too easy, doesn't it? Of course it does, because we've been taught since we could walk that life is hard. And we believed it, so we thought it, and then we experienced it, and the belief was reinforced. And life has become hard—thank goodness. (Thank goodness our thoughts are so unfailing and predictable!) And thank goodness that making a change couldn't possibly be easier. Just think it and let your destiny unfold.

YOUR NAME WAS WHISPERED

Your name was whispered
before you were born,
and as if from the mist,
your image took form.
The Spirit of Life
had begun its quest
to know of itself
through the ultimate test:
A Being of Light
set free in creation
to master the gift
of imagination.

And you're passing that test with flying colors! You already realize that it's a magical world you live in. You're beginning to see that the life you lead is packed with daily miracles.

And you're taking responsibility for all of the good and bad that you've ever experienced. Most critically, though, you're beginning to realize that your thoughts have become the "things" of your life, and you realize, too, that this will not change, ever.

You are master of your imagination, and your imagination is master over your matter. You are the gatekeeper to the abundance, joy, and prosperity that now awaits your beck and call. It is that easy. The test, however, is to know it.

You are an unlimited Being of Light, and you know it.

HEAVEN'S GATE

What's the hurry?
The world will wait!
There's no need to rush
before heaven's gate.

You now stand before Heaven's Gate. Not because you face death, but because you face life. Not in some deep, abstract sense, but in the here and now.

In all of reality, from everywhere that's ever been thought of, physical and spiritual, to the center of this very earth and stretching out to the ends of time, there is only heaven. And to get a really good idea of what it looks like, just stop what you're doing and look around. Look out the window. Look down the street. Look at a tree. And look into the sky.

Understand, too, that you are at the center of your own experience. And just as you can choose what you'll be doing after reading this, so can you choose how you will feel and what you will think. So, too, can you choose how the rest of your life will unfold in a kingdom you rule with the thoughts you choose to think.

Nothing could possibly be better, or easier, than the way it already is here and now. You stand before Heaven's Gate—just know it and walk through.

IT'S ALL ABOUT YOU

The world is your oyster
and life is your ocean,
just follow your heart
to set the waves into motion.

It's all about you! You are the reason the birds sing. You are the reason the flowers bloom. And you are the reason the sun rises each day: you, just as you are, flaws and all, sinner or saint.

It's all about you because it's all for you, and it's all for you because it's all of you. You are the dream weaver that spun this tale into being. And you are the sorcerer that breathed life into voids where there had been none. And now, after too long a sleep, you tiptoe through the tulips, afraid you'll disturb them. You bow before life lest you be seen as imperfect, and you inch through days you feel unworthy to keep.

But if only you'd awaken to the truth that it's all here for you, that the tulips long for the passing of your shadow, the sun yearns to see the smile on your face, and the earth aches to feel your carefree steps.

The world is your oyster! Set the waves in motion! The tulips too! They're all about you! You are so worthy!

NICE SPLASH

In this journey called life,
I know in my heart
that, be it ever so humble,
I'm glad for my part.

It's easy to think that if you weren't, someone else would be in your place, doing what you do. But no one will ever be able to do what you do.

Every acquaintance you greet, every phone you answer, every pet you pamper, and every smile, wave, wink, and hug in your life would never happen without you. Your every move ripples across humanity to places, people, and souls you don't consciously know of.

In the pond of time and space, each one of us hits the water every moment of every day. And I can see your splash from here! Remember: *Thoughts Become Things.*

YOU ARE INVINCIBLE

*Let me walk
with my own self
in a wondrous, glorious dream.
And down this path
that we shall tread,
we'll be an invincible team.*

You know, you're pretty incredible! Probably one in a zillion if someone counted. Really. You feel things so intensely, you wear your heart on your sleeve, and you care deeply about what's right and good. So let me ask you, why are you so hard on yourself? You're much more tolerant of others who are far less enlightened, but for yourself, you raise the bar. Not fair!

You see, the more you like yourself, the more everyone else will like you.

And that's not even the half of it! The more you like yourself, the easier everything gets. You become more in demand at work, at home, and everywhere else. Your health improves. Your "balance" improves. Abundance effortlessly flows to you. You worry less. You play more. You fear less. You know more. You even get better looking! Minutes and hours are actually added to your days. Life gets better, and then ... you've got momentum. You're on a roll. You can't be stopped.

Evidence everywhere is mounting. There's no doubt about it; life is soooo grand! And you? You are invincible.

LIFE NEEDS YOU

Cast your fears
into the sea.
Life needs you, dear,
entirely.

To get a handle on your fears, embrace them. Look them in the eye. Love and understand them and be set free. You've given them birth, and you've given them a reason to be in your life. Seek out that reason. Why are you really afraid? What are you really afraid of? How could it be possible for you to imagine that you, of such divine heritage, might not prevail? How could you ever believe that you might lose anything considering your eternal nature? And how might you have ever come to believe that your happiness was dependent upon something or someone outside of you? When you see yourself as you truly are—unlimited, forever, and abundant—fears and doubts will no longer cling to you for their meaning, and your natural confidence, joy, and harmony will reign supreme.

Life needs you. We all need you.

W ould you ever worry again, if you absolutely knew—really, really knew—that you've made no mistakes?

That no matter what challenges have come your way or may come your way, all will add to your joy in the morrow?

That all you have to do to live the life of your dreams is make the decision?

That you've already made the difference in the world that you now hope to make?

That one day, everything will make perfect sense and you'll be glad for all of it?

That everyone will eventually know the truth?

That you will live forever?

That there is no hell and no judgment apart from what we dish out to ourselves?

That you are now adored more than you can possibly comprehend?

That new friends and the happiest of times lie ahead?

It's time you knew!

THE SPIRIT OF LIFE

In the depths of space
there isn't a trace
of the power that brought
it to be.
But it cannot hide
if you look inside;
it was the Spirit of Life
set free.

Within you lies the answer to your every question, the key to your happiness, and the memory of your true divinity. It's tempting to think that you might find these things from outside events or people, but the events of your life are mere stepping stones on a path you've prepared for your own awakenings, and your friends simply reflect who you think you are at any given point, not necessarily who you really are.

On your journey through the heavenly landscapes of time and space, you walk in love, but you've chosen to walk alone—willingly severed from the recollection of your "oneness" with all awareness and the knowledge that your dreams have already come true. For how else could you experience your omniscience had you not created a reality where its presence was veiled in a paradise cloaked in matter?

Here you're driven by your burning desires to experience how magnificent you are. All you need to be happy, healthy, wealthy, and wise lies within. You are the Spirit of Life set free.

FANTASTIC VOYAGE

Do not judge the journey
by the path you're now on.

L ike driving cross-country, you can't possibly know in advance if or where you may encounter detours, hairpin turns, or passing cars with noses and whatnot pressed to the window.

Moreover, little if any of the scenery you travel through will remotely resemble the destination you have in mind. Yet neither the constellations you see nor the unexpected maneuvers you take will ever mean you aren't headed exactly where you want to go, moving as swiftly as possible, getting closer every flippin' day.

WHICH HAT YOU WEAR

It's not what you do.
It's who you are.

Your part is bigger than you can now possibly imagine. It matters little what your job is or isn't. Who you know or don't know. What degrees you have or don't have. What you would have, could have, or should have done. What matters is that you are here! A being whose mere thoughts, feelings, and emotions give birth to worlds, adding endless possibilities and dimensions to a Universe forever expanding. Your every concern and kindness sets waves into motion that never, ever cease. In the symphony of humankind, every one of us makes a difference. And while this may not seem so evident as you play your part, your absence would be suffered by all, in times and places beyond comprehension.

Everything is important, everything matters, and the world is and will be a better place simply because you were here.

Indeed.

THE BEST THINGS ARE FREE

*A dolphin smiles
because it's happy to be
alive in a world
where the best things are free.*

Living in a world of illusions, have you ever stopped to wonder what is real here? Most of us grew up thinking that material things like rocks, bicycles, our bodies, and planets are real, but things like our thoughts, emotions, and imagination are not. Somehow, we got it backwards.

Our spiritual selves and the journey we're on are real. Our essence and our experiences, and those elements that define both, like our beliefs, emotions, desires, and values, are real—the intangibles. We're born of illusion, into illusion, so that we can feel what is real.

So why does a dolphin smile? For the same reasons that you can choose to! Because the things that we all really want—to be happy, to feel fulfilled, to love and be loved—are abundantly free and have nothing to do with the material stuff that seemingly motivates us. And not only are they free, but we give them to ourselves when we think we're deserving enough, or we've paid a high enough price, or sacrificed enough, or suffered enough.

You are deserving enough! You've paid your dues, and sacrifice and suffering were never meant to be part of the picture. Today, there will be hundreds of reasons to feel all the things you most want to feel.

Just give them to yourself!

58

In your deepest thoughts, what might you imagine is the end game to being consciously aware? The highest ideal?

Finding love? Maybe, but love is also the beginning and mid-game. It's the given. Inescapable. Love is not so much a reason as it is the medium of any reality.

Finding God? Maybe, though God's never been lost.

Finding self? Maybe, but you're not really lost either.

Learning? Maybe, but learning is valuable for a reason; it's not a reason in and of itself.

What then? What else is there? So simple …

Happiness! If anything, that is the endgame. And perhaps no other variable in your life today is as important.

Follow your heart.

THE VOYAGE

Your dreams are gifts
that set you in motion
on the tides of time
where life is an ocean.
And your sails are filled
with the winds of desire
to surge through the waves
of murk and mire.
But when you awaken
with your goal at hand,
you'll see your true destination
was the voyage not the land.

Have a dream? A burning desire? If you're breathing, you do! And they're laden with treasure, though not as you might expect. It's the journeys they inspire and the

territory they'll unexpectedly draw you through that will be your reward for their pursuit—even more so than their ultimate realization.

A lifetime is made up of journeys, not destinations. And to be happiest, one must enjoy the ride, even though during it you will not have whatever it is you're after, or you wouldn't be on the journey to begin with. By being happy with what you do have, where you've been, and especially with who you are, the journey can be savored because you'll worry less about exactly where it's taking you and focus more on the unending miracle that is you and your life.

We're sorry to have interrupted your journey simply to remind you that it is a journey. But we trust you'll understand and that you'll take a moment to realize that while you'll likely always be after something you don't have (which is perfectly OK), as you learn to enjoy the voyage, you'll come to see that your dreams and desires are indeed the gifts that set you in motion on a journey unfolding right here and now.

BEEN THERE, DONE THAT

Once a "mistake,"
twice you're cool.

The thing about goals and resolutions is that they kick your brain into maximum overdrive, comparing where and who you are today with where and who you want to be. And you start thinking, "Sheeez, how the heck am I going to do that?" Well, before you answer, realize that this question is at the root of most every mortal "ill," from stress and sleepless nights to ulcers and cancer.

Think back to every major and wonderful breakthrough or accomplishment you've ever experienced: meeting someone really special, getting that impossible-to-get job, averting a disaster, clutching in a crunch, winning whatever you've won, and discovering your niche, your home, a best friend. And then

remember what initially led you to each and every one. Wasn't it always some sort of unpredictable twist of fate? A "coincidence" or an "accident" of some kind. Right? Right! Always.

Now, realize this isn't just true for you; it's true for everyone. Always has been. We know what we want. We do what we can. If our beliefs permit, we endlessly daydream of the end result.

And then... and then...

Yes, then! The Universe is engaged! And lo and behold, the unexpected falls in our laps when we're not looking and our thoughts become things.

Since this is the way of the world, please incorporate it into your thinking. Stop the nonsense of trying to figure it all out. The ultimate means of goal manifestation are beyond our comprehension, so don't go there. Believe in the magic of life; expect miracles and count on them. This isn't a stretch.

They have been happening all your life. And from now on, every morning, get yourself out of bed with the thought that something unpredictably wonderful is about to happen! Something beyond your ability to calculate! And it will, as it always has. It must. It's the law.

THE POWER OF WORRY

*When you catch yourself thinking something you don't like,
stop it; reverse it; set yourself free.*

What happens when someone worries?
Basically, they think of a hundred reasons why something might go wrong. And all of those thoughts then struggle to become things, sometimes overriding their more constructive thoughts.

It's like a train wreck. It ain't pretty, but that's the power of worry.

Now, let's say you want something fantastic to manifest in your life.

Hypothetically, let's say you want even more laughter and another beautiful home. Have you sat down yet and listed a hundred reasons why it might come to you easily, fast, and harmoniously?

I think you should.

Today works.

THE MOST AMAZING WORLD OF UNENDING WONDERS

Can't get it?
Don't sweat it;
let it come to you!
If it's right
and you hold tight,
your dreams will all come true!

You already know that worrying only fouls things up, but why? Because thoughts become things! And if your thoughts include doubt, it means you're able to visualize and see things happening in your life that you don't want to happen. And as soon as you can mentally see them, their reality (in the world of thoughts) emerges and they immediately begin striving to become part of your time-space life. And the more you think any thoughts, right or wrong, good or bad, especially

when you feel them as you think them, the closer they get to becoming things.

So you set the stage for a battle when you also think thoughts contrary to whatever it is you want. And it'll be the thoughts you think and feel the most that you'll ultimately experience in the flesh. Although if you allow the battle to wage a long time, you may seem to get neither. Stagnation! Whereas, if all you think of are the things that you want, then their reality will literally come to you, because they'll be the only possible future you've created. It's so simple! You always get what you think about. That's how things work in this most amazing world of unending wonders. And when you really understand this, it will become very, very difficult for you to worry about, much less conceive of, a possible future containing undesirable things.

What's meant to be? Absolutely nothing, except for the reality, the future, that you choose to focus on. Think happy thoughts, and you are "meant" to have happiness. Think life is hard, and it will be. Think thoughts of abundance, and you'll experience luxe! This isn't something that will start working once you believe in it; it's the law. It's how things already work in time and space, and it's the game you came here to master. So even when circumstances say, "No way," hold fast to your dreams and their occurrence will become inevitable.

Of course, beliefs, actions, and words play a role, too—a powerful role. But at the end of the day, the thoughts you think the most—which will inevitably be the ones you believe in and unavoidably move toward—will become the things and events of your life.

Thank goodness!

ASK YOURSELF

*The mysteries of your soul begin
to show themselves when you look within.*

Got a question? About life? About work? About love? About your past, present, or future?

Very likely there are lots of great people in your life you can turn to for answers, but none know you like you know you! And none are as wise to the ways and the needs and the dreams and the desires that are your own as you are. Neither could another know of your greatest potentials nor of the promises life has in store for you.

Daily, in moments of quiet, ask yourself for the direction you seek and look for the answers in your feelings and intuitions. Listen, too, to your mind. The right way will feel good and make sense. Expect answers!

There's a little bit of everyone inside of you, and there's a little bit of you inside of all others. Humanity's greatest and most vile potentials lie within each of us. By understanding what motivates us to act kindly or with malice, we can begin asking questions about the behavior of others. And with understanding, we can begin loving—not their behavior, but their potential; not their decisions, but their journey. And with love, we can begin healing by example, showing kindness, compassion, and another way.

MANIPULATION

*Over the moon
and past the stars,
when you dream with a friend
you fly twice as far.*

Want to know a scary truth about the power of thought? Thoughts can actually manipulate the people in your life.

Now, this isn't a bad thing, and I'm not suggesting you try to change someone who doesn't want to be changed (that's impossible), but there is a "whole ton" of people out there, hordes even, who want exactly what corresponds to you getting your way. Essentially, they want what you want but for their own reasons. And your thoughts, when clear and unfettered by limiting beliefs, reach out to these people and literally begin changing their behavior, drawing them closer and closer and closer to your life.

How? Realities are actually switched around, like a train jumping tracks, in ways that are invisible to the physical senses until after the change has happened. And then, presto, they're there.

Who? Friends, lovers, customers, employers, employees, agents, partners, associates, manufacturers, publishers, directors, deal makers, or any kind of cohort you could possibly imagine.

The trick is not to try to manipulate any specific someone but to maintain a clear focus upon your goal so that all others can clearly hear your calling.

Another trick is never underestimating the power of your thoughts.

IN THE JUNGLE

In the jungle there's a secret
that all the animals keep,
and in the ocean it's no different,
their code runs just as deep:
Whether the hunter or the hunted,
your fate is just as grand,
because in the final hour
you'll meet again as planned.
For neither is the victor—
they just fulfill the plan,
and the same is true of people,
each does the best they can.

Have you ever wondered how you might behave if you were in someone else's shoes? If you have, you'll likely admit that this kind of thinking is usually critical of the person you're thinking about. The truth is, you are the other person, and they are behaving exactly as you would if you were indeed in the exact same shoes. You might say that others show us what we, too, would do if in their shoes—however inconsiderate, abusive, outrageous, or immoral their behavior is.

True, you are probably more thoughtful, fearless, loving, and honest than those who disappoint you. But you are also at a different point in your journey, maybe "more advanced," or maybe just more at ease for having chosen a less "challenging" path. We're all of "one," exhibiting different colors of the same light, and rather than passing judgment, it's best to remember that each of us is just doing the best we can.

MY FRIEND

I've started a journey
I'll see through to the end.
And I'm ever so grateful
it includes you,
my friend.

A friend is forever and so is their effect on your life. Friends affect how you think about yourself and your place in time and space, and how you think changes everything.

A friend is someone whose unspoken approval and appreciation for your company helps you to remember your own grace and beauty.

A fellow adventurer who takes pride in having made your acquaintance.

A pilgrim on his way to a promised land who has made time to be with you.

A giver whose kindness and honesty helps light your way on darker days.

A wayfarer learning to love unconditionally.

And you're an awesome friend!

You've always "been," and from the vastness from which you sprang, you've paved your way with friendships that will always "be." Even in your solitude, even right now, you are surrounded by unseen friends who rally around you with love, understanding, and appreciation for the exact person you are today. You have no idea how popular you really are.

IT'S A MIRACLE!

M-*agically*
I-*ncited*
R-*eality*
A-*djustment*
C-*oncealed by*
L-*oving*
E-*ntities*

The truth is, nothing you do is short of miraculous. So why is it that some of the things you do, you let the Universe do for you effortlessly, while other things you do, you insist on doing alone with clenched teeth, sweat, and self-criticism? Why do you only trust the Universe to grow your cells, beat your heart, and finish the sentences you start, when it's just as capable of helping you live in abundance, find love, feel peace, and achieve goals? The bigger truth is that all of those things are done by the Universe anyway. Yet we think that we must do them ourselves, alone.

So fess up, set your goals, and understand that there's a process bigger than you. Visualize, move, trust, and let the Universe take over. Could it be any easier?

There are only miracles—especially when we get out of their way!

DON'T LOOK BACK

Born of imagination,
your thoughts are things
with magical powers
that know how to bring
your dreams to life ...
and your nightmares, too!
So watch what you think
or it could happen to you.

And what of those mysterious thoughts of yours that have brought you to here and now?

Don't look back! No matter what decisions you've made in your past, they were the right ones for your greater fulfillment and for the fulfillment of those affected.

Right at this very moment, the Universe is now conspiring, at full throttle, to make all your dreams come true from where you are today. It hasn't given up nor should you— hypothetically, you know. It hasn't judged you nor should you. Help the Universe out here. It's still aiming for all the fun that lies ahead! So you may as well make the best of wherever you are today and keep focusing on where you want to go, not where you've been.

Some time ago you were given dominion over all things. And you've still got it.

FOR THE LOVE OF THE GAME

The secret of life
is not to resist
but to ride the tide
in search of your bliss.

Just because you can do anything, have anything, and be anything doesn't mean you have to be the biggest, fastest, skinniest, richest chick in the henhouse. Talk about angst, stress, and resistance!

Besides, happiness doesn't begin with the "home run." It begins with a love of the "game"—from which home runs happen automatically.

Tallyho, and as you choose your games, enjoy the trek to first base.

THE DISTANCE BETWEEN HERE AND THERE

Mind over matter,
and limitations shatter.

What is it that you really, really want? And what's keeping you from it? What is it that lies between where you want to be and where you are now? What is it that stands between the person that you are today and the person that you most want to be?

Now, it's not a someone, and it's not a something. It's not your circumstances, and it's not your job. It's not your childhood or even your kids. And it's definitely not fate or karma. It's your thoughts. In particular, the thoughts of yours that do not include your wished-for reality in their images of who you are today. The ones hiding behind a fear or two that see your dreams coming true in the future instead of the present.

The ones that secretly affirm, "Not here, not now, not yet. I'm not ready!"

Thank goodness it's not a "reality thing" that's left you "without." Thank goodness it's just a matter of your thoughts. Your thoughts! Because those, heck, those are yours, and you can change them today. Just think new ones, like the kind that say "I am," or "Right now," or something like "Thank you, Universe, that it is already done!"

You are a creative adventurer zooming through time and space, endowed with the power to think new thoughts, even while facing circumstances that would have you think otherwise.

Whatever it is that you really want lies only a thought away. A thought of yours.

That's it. That's all. Nothing else matters. There are no maybes, no ifs, no mitigating factors. Not karma, not fate, not luck.

No matter what you want to have, do, or be, the Universe has to give it to you if you hold on to and move with those thoughts. It's the law, and your entire life has been the proof.

As Good as It Gets

*Move through your doubts
and get past your tears.
Paradise lingers
just beyond all your fears.*

How would paradise look to you? Would there be lots of smiles and laughter, abundance and plenty, kindness and thanksgiving, peace and goodwill, health and harmony, love and joy? Would there be a worry in sight?

Did you notice that all of those elements, every single one of them, exist on earth, here and now? Moreover, is there a single thing in that list that hasn't, at one point or another, existed in your life and times? There's no denying it; at some point in your life you've touched paradise. And chances are just as good, if you keep your eyes peeled as this week unfolds, you'll notice that you're there right now.

This is as good as it gets. You make the difference.

Yo Ho Ho!
It's Time to Have Fun!

*Time and space
aren't quite as they seem,
just magical props
in a magical dream.*

And now, mid-dream, you realize you're dreaming. But you think it can't possibly be a dream because it's all so real. The birds are singing, the trees are swaying, your computer is humming, and the colors everywhere dazzle. It couldn't be a dream! But you know it is.

Well, if this is a dream, here are three penetrating questions to ask: Who's the dreamer? Where does the dreamer want the dream to go? And how do you manipulate the things and events of a dream to get to where you want to go?

All dreams are adventures, and the most adventurous of all dreams is the one we're living right here and now—called life.

BELIEVE IT

I am ... anything I choose to be!

And how do you become whatever it is you now choose to be? By knowing that you already are whatever it is you now choose to be. By believing. By visualizing that your desires have already been fulfilled in a fantasized past. Not by focusing on the desire or on the future.

If you focus on desire, you get desire, which is fulfilled by creating a life that is void of the things you want. If you focus on the future, you reinforce that your present is without the things you want, and this focus will bring you more of the same—an unfulfilled present.

Act as if you already are whatever it is you "used to" want to become, and it shall be done!

Is bad luck any less a creation than good fortune? Is a one-dollar bill any less a manifestation than a hundred-dollar bill? Is disease any less a miracle than health?

They're all the same—just different brush strokes on the canvas of life. And you get to choose yours, based upon what you think of as practical, reasonable, and likely.

Go for the full monty! After all, it requires the exact same amount of paint.

WHAT COULD BE EASIER?

It's the little things you do
that make the big things happen.

What you physcially do clarifies desire, evidences faith, and demonstrates belief. All of which whip the entire Universe into service on your behalf, commanding destiny, summoning fortune, and orchestrating the magic.

Just begin and prepare to be astounded.

THE WAY

There are times when you stumble
and there are times when you're lost,
but to get where you're going,
these are well worth their cost.

O nly when pressed with darkness can you begin to seek
the light. And how could you understand your authority
if you had not first relinquished it? How could you find your
way if you had not first strayed? Now, your experiments with
darkness, limits, and fear have long outgrown their use. It's time
to wake up, to remember, to know that you are far more than
the role you've been playing.

You are the light, the power, the way for which all things are
possible.

EXPRESS SERVICE

Daily,
hour by hour,
minute by minute,
second by second,
you are admired by eyes in the unseen.

You're sitting comfortably, confidently, gazing at the hustle and bustle of a busy train station platform beneath you. The excitement and energy is amazing—people coming and going to and fro, their journeys about to begin—yet at times it's overwhelming. Happily, deep down, you know your own train is going to take you to friends and laughter, wealth and abundance, peace and harmony. And knowing this, you are calm, easily able to doze when the frenzy seems too much, content to be patient for as long as it takes.

Minutes pass ... hours ... days ... You begin to get restless. There's something you're forgetting.

Every time you awaken you see from your vantage point a platform swarming with people, like bees in a hive. Everyone has somewhere to go and an all-important train to catch, except, it seems, yourself. And as you ponder this in bewilderment, you scare yourself even more by realizing that you have no idea what your train will look like. Scarier still, you start to wonder if, perhaps, it's already come. You start to panic.

Just then you notice a kindly old soul who's been sitting beside you for as long as you can remember, and in that moment, you understand

that at some forgotten level of awareness, the two of you are very dear friends. As if prompted, before you can even speak, and with the most reassuring smile you've ever seen in your life, your friend explains that you've been watching all the platform activity from the first-class comfort of your own private coach high above the tracks. Dozing before departing from each station and awakening just as the wheels screeched to a halt at the next, in a journey the two of you had quite thoroughly planned long before the beginning of time.

You're well on your way, exactly where and who you dreamed you'd be, riding first-class in a cabin that's the envy of many.

RUN FOR YOUR LIFE!

*Escape the ordinary,
and run for your life.
Let go of your fears,
and let your dreams take flight!*

Fear simply marks the absence of understanding. Are you worried about your business or your financial affairs? Then remember that new customers, earnings, and cash flow come from abundant thinking and "right" actions, not market studies, statistics, and trends.

Are you afraid of the unknown? Then simply remember that all good in your life and in the lives of those you love first emerged from the unknown.

Are you worried about love? Then you've forgotten that it embraces you even now; that it doesn't come from a person or a place but emanates from within; that it will soothe and comfort, as soon as you let it, in the form and substance that most pleases you. Claim it now, hold on, and expect it unquestioningly.

A PRESENT FOR YOU

To most, I'm a face
lost in the race.
But really,
I've already won!

What do people think about you? That you're cool, that you're lazy, that you're happy or sad, that you're creative, stubborn, passive, aggressive, determined, generous, or selfish? Of course, all that matters is what you think about you. But you expected me to say that.

Here's a new thought: Whatever someone else thinks about you contains truth. Whether they're motivated by love or pain, it doesn't matter, and whether they're right or wrong is irrelevant. It's their truth, and for the fact that this person is in your life (immediately or distantly) and that you're aware of their feelings, consider their perspective a gift—one worthy of exploration until you find peace with it. It may even be why you were drawn together.

OMENS OF ADVENTURE

Do you want to:
Tap into all the knowledge that's ever been known?
Travel out-of-body through time and space?
Walk on water? Read minds? Speak tongues?
Love yourself? Feel good? Enjoy today?

Yeah, let's start at the bottom and work up.

If you understood the extraordinary gifts every single challenge in your life makes possible—even inevitable—you'd celebrate your challenges, new and old alike, as the omens that they are of new beginnings, spectacular change, and enhanced superpowers.

What a system, huh?

CHOOSING CHANGE

In case you haven't caught on:
You are not where you now think you are.
You are not what you now think you are.
You are not even who you now think you are.

When desirous of a life change, or any kind of a change, it's wiser to start from a place of, "I am who I am today, where I am today, because this was my choice and it has served me well. However, it no longer serves me. My choices have changed, and I give thanks for the amazing transformational energies that now sweep through my amazing life."

This is better than, "I don't know how I got here. I hate this. I must be sabotaging my own progress. I just won't accept things as they are anymore. I'm desperate for a change. By this time next year, my life will totally rock!"

OK?

You don't even have to remember the choices that led you to this day, but by understanding you made them, the kingdom, the power, and the glory knowingly become yours.

TRAILBLAZER

As many fish as there are in the sea,
there's none I'd rather be than me!

What a priceless view of the world you have, and what precious jewels you add to the "Crown of One" with your unique and penetrating insights. You know, you might sometimes take yourself for granted, but there are those whose lives you touch who never will, and then their lives will touch others, and so on and so on and so on, beyond count, beyond time.

So, let us bow and sing your praise, for all our lives are made better by yours.

Not a one of us was cut out for the challenges and dreams you've chosen to take on. You and you alone are the able one. And now you tread where none have tread before. The trail you're blazing is opening up the road for others; for when any one of us meets a challenge or achieves a goal, we've broken down barriers and cleared the way for all.

So when you dream, there are others who dream with you. You're not alone—not when you struggle and not when you soar. Plus, the longer you hold on, the more time you give your friends to add to your momentum.

THE NAME OF THE GAME

Far out in the ocean
on a moonlit night,
a circle of dolphins
slips out of sight.
They're on a mission
of the grandest scale—
to spread the word
to every minnow and whale
that life's an illusion
just waiting for you
to believe in your dreams
so they can come true.

I t's not supposed to be hard. It's not supposed to be easy. It's not supposed to be anything until you say it is, until you believe it is! And that is the name of the game! Win it and dominion is granted, the world is your oyster, and providence becomes play without all the sweat, blood, tears, and years you've been led to believe are requisites.

One day soon, you will see that nothing could possibly be easier! And boy will you laugh!

THE SYSTEM WORKS

Imagine it.
Move towards it.
Has to happen.
It always works.

And then, all of a sudden … you're on top of the world, an overnight sensation, the cause of intergalactic jubilation. What seemed like unending preparation has now culminated in your delivery. You can do no wrong; your vision is clear; your mission divinely inspired. Smiles, laughter, and accolades surround you. Friends, family, and loved ones salute you. The time is right, the place chosen, and the ultimate test is about to begin. You're ready.

As if struck by lightning, the scene instantly changes. The next thing you know you're a wee little babe and all the festivities become a distant blur. The images and vibrations of "the party to end all parties" rapidly fade away, while the songs and laughter still ringing in your ears are replaced with harsh voices and loud speakers. Strangers surround you, and what you had felt as an indescribable lightness of being has been replaced with gravity.

"NOTHING, absolutely NOTHING, could be worth this. There has to be a mistake. Something must have gone wrong."

In total shock and broken-hearted, alone and frightened, you hear a calm voice rising above the ruckus. Warm hands are now drawing you through the air, holding you safely. As the motion gently stops, you hear words that cause every cell of your body to ring with vitality, recalling the preparations that made this all possible; confirming the clarity of your earlier convictions; reminding you of countless agreements, treaties, and rendezvous plans; and instilling within your heart a vision of the perfection, love, and purpose you were born of.

"My dearest, welcome to the world. We've been waiting for this day such a long, lo-o-ong time."

Then, without logic or rationale you "think" your reply, in words as alien to you as the artificial light in your room, "Me too."

And while this experience passes swiftly and you quickly forget all that the calm voice evoked, it imparted a confidence that will never again leave you and a remembrance that all is well, that everything is going to be forever OK, and that you are here because it's where you most wanted to be, in a world that most wanted to have you.

BLA-A-AGH

Everything's gonna B.O.K.

No matter who you are, no matter where you are, no matter what your issues, no matter what, everything will always end up OK. And just as profound, whether or not it's now apparent, everything already is OK. Right here and now! How adventurous would life be if we were "challenge-free"? If we all had perfect bodies, perfect self-esteem, and lived cushy little lives? Bla-a-agh!

But what if, painful as they may temporarily be, we could litter "the course" with obstacles on the sole condition that they could all be overcome? What if the playing field held the potential for the realization of our greatest hopes and dreams? What if no single peril we might face was insurmountable? Hmmm. What a concept! But definitely not for every celestial

couch potato. This concept is suited only to adventurers—and perfect for you!

Besides, what could you possibly worry about once you realize that there are still ever more sunrises to come? More songbirds to hear and more flowers to pick? Walks to take and sand castles to make? Aromas wafting, music haunting, and sites to see?

Come what may, the best things in life will remain free. And the Universe will still count you as a favorite child with whom it is most pleased.

Stay the course! Because not only will the beauty and the truth always remain, but you will get there! You will arrive! Your day will come! And no misfortune, setback, or mistake can ever change this.

BECAUSE I LOVE YOU

The answer to every question beginning with "why"
begins with, "Because I love you."
And the answer to every question beginning with "how"
begins with, "None of your beeswax."

"So," the little bird asked the big bird, "This is heaven?"

"No, no, my dear. The skies you flew in before you arrived here from earth, that was heaven. This? This is just home, from whence all get to choose their next heaven."

"Earth heaven? It didn't feel like heaven! I didn't see heaven!"

"Did you look?"

"N-No, because they, everyone, told me heaven was next!"

"And you believed them?"

"Well, it was so hard, so scary, so lonely."

"Was it always that way?"

"N-No. Not always. But when it wasn't for me, it was for someone else!"

"You'd have preferred?"

"Friends galore! Laughter every day! Challenges I could handle! Abundance I could spend! Health I could use! And, well, incredible you-know-what."

"But you had all that, didn't you? And more."

"Oh."

"Yes, oh."

"But not all the time, day in, day out, served on a silver platter!"

"Well, believe it or not, little friend, that would have been hell."

Birds talking about heaven. Funny, huh?

DON'T DO IT

In this greatest of all adventures,
you cannot ever be less than
you really are: limitless,
forever, and totally awesome.
But you can think that you are less
than you really are. Don't!

There are very, very, very few don'ts in this kingdom of thoughts. But seeing yourself as less than you really are should be one of them. Actually, there are just as few should bes in this kingdom, too. Let's keep it that way!

What if you were born as healthy, wealthy, and wise as you now dream of becoming?

Or what if you didn't have any of the challenges you now face?

If this were the case, you wouldn't be a fraction of the person that you already are today.

There's a reason to the madness, a reason you sometimes feel trapped, stuck, fallen, and bruised. And it has everything to do with the enlightenment you sought and the triumphs that are only now possible. You wanted more—more than having everything handed to you on a silver platter—and you got it. And this makes all the difference.

Angels sing your name.

FEAR THIS!

*If all of the people
in all of the world
could turn their worries
into laughter,
then all of the people
in all of the world
would live happily ever after.*

Oh, don't torture yourself! It does no good. Don't give such ridiculous importance to those things that you don't want to happen. No detour or setback you may ever encounter will keep you from where you're going: to a land of plenty, to a time of bliss, to a place of laughter, friends, and love. Your every cup will runneth over.

Nothing before you can take years away from eternity, make the Universe less, or dim the Being of Light that you will always be. You are so magnificent, you have no idea. And the fact that you don't remember it doesn't change it. No matter what happens, you will prevail. And you'll be happy for those challenges you placed in your way so that you could again experience how divine you are.

ALL THEY NEED IS YOU

Every dream you dream
will one day come true.
So dream your dreams—
all they need is you.

Y ou provide the spark, the Universe will set the fire, and it
will rage in every color you can imagine but no more. And
it will last for as long as you can see it lasting but no longer.
And it will light the darkest corners of the world if you ask it
to. But there'll be no flame at all, not even the faintest flicker, if
you don't first dream.

All that stands between you and your unrealized dreams is
the dreaming.

I t's true! It's true! No matter how high or low you're feeling today, right now, behind the scenes, an adoring Universe
and invisible friends are busy at work. Your dreams have been
caught, as if by sails in the heavens, and are now being har-
nessed by an able crew to navigate into the time and space
before you.

Circumstances are being forged. Facts and figures are
being calculated. Players are being placed. And whenever necessary, rules are being bent. But just as
sails depend on an ever present wind, so
does your crew depend on a captain who
will persevere.

Land ho!

GET JIGGY!

To dwell upon what might have been
is perhaps the greatest sin.

Whoa, no way, don't look back! Before you, just up ahead, lies forever. It's a sparkling, magical time and place filled with smiles, laughter, and new friends. A place filled with second chances and new circumstances, where every dream you've ever dreamt will—and already has—come true. A place of endless discovery, boundless potential, and blissful peace. It's opulent, it's colorful, and it's easy. It's sunny, shady, and breezy. Happy, carefree, and infinite, and you're going to be there for a really, really, really long time. So lighten up, get over it, look ahead, and get jiggy!

And don't you know it? Yet you still look back! Well, next time you do, give yourself some credit. All things considered, you did a great job. You did your best, given what was then your understanding of life. And because of where you've been, conditions are now perfect; you're poised for greatness! Everything that had to be learned, you learned. You're now ready, willing, and able. And oh, my gosh, you're going to be so happy!

FORBIDDEN FRUIT

Blessed are emotions,
for though some make you weep,
you're better to have known them
for the secrets that they keep.

Like limiting beliefs, unpleasant emotions can all be traced back to the original sin, the forbidden fruit we eat of everyday.

The original sin was believing that the things of time and space were more real than spirit, that time and space precede spirit, instead of understanding that it works the other way around. And ever since then, we've been susceptible to the emotions that arise from our perceptions of loss, separation, powerlessness, limitedness, and more, all from the belief that we are merely human beings—a very false belief!

Realizing this, and understanding that you are indeed an unlimited Being of Light—eternal, powerful, one with the Universe—your limiting beliefs have to give way to the light of truth. And at this point, the emotions of happiness, peace, and fulfillment must flood your awareness.

You've Arrived

If I had only known
just how well I'd really do,
the journey would have mattered;
instead, alas, it's through.
And don't you really know it,
that in the end you'll say:
I'd trade this pot of gold
for another single day.

Y ou are a success! You have succeeded! Give credit where credit is due. It's time to enjoy the view, to hear the music, to smell the flowers, to walk tall and love it all. You've earned it! And you deserve to coast.

CURIOUS CUMULONIMBUS

If you can see a cloud, it can see you.
Same for trees.
And beauty.
Kind of makes you want to get out more, huh?

Wouldn't it be nice to meet a kind, old messiah, who, sitting crossed-legged under the shade of a mighty oak next to a babbling brook, greeted you with a penetrating smile, kind eyes, and tears running down his face, saying, "At last. I've waited most of my life for this moment, for the chance to fulfill the prophecy, to share the journey, and to bask in your loveliness before I pass you the baton"?

"Me?!"

"Yes, you! The chosen one. Holiest of the holies, sacred among the sacred. Haven't you always sensed your deeper purpose? Haven't you always marveled at your own insights?

Haven't you wondered at the countless miracles that have sprung up in your midst?

"The time is nigh that you will spread your wings and soar so high that the rest of the world might notice, to live the truths that have been whispered into your ear as you rode great clouds in your sleep, to be an example of what love can do, to demonstrate the powers of thought and expectation, and to join with other Light Workers in this celebration of creation called life."

Well … I'm sure it would be nice, but we're kind of running out of time … will this passage do?

LIFE WORKS

I'm through with pleasing everyone.
I'm done with fooling me.
It's time I started living life
the way I want it to be.

Be ever so careful with this one! Indeed, it's high time you followed your heart and honored your preferences. But first asking why you want what you want may save you one thousand false starts.

Is the reason to have fun, to be happy, or to grow? Or is it to redeem, to prove, or to show? It's an especially important question when it seems life isn't working, because the truth is, life always works.

Dang it!

Unending Miracles

There are only miracles.

Hmmm—that one likely missed you. Sure, you believe it and all, and you're probably thinking that you already know that life, and every moment of it, is precious and miraculous, but then what? Oh, I think I know. Somewhere along your journey you began to think of yourself as the byproduct of this incredible miracle—like foam is to the sea. Well, if I may, let me point out a few things:

In this Universe, thought rules! It's the prime mover. It can tear down barriers or erect them. It can open doors or close them. It can build hope or dash dreams. It can make friends or enemies. It can produce wealth or poverty, health or illness. But thoughts can do nothing until they're thought, which is where you come in. Today, you get to think whatever you want, which puts you at the epicenter of this incredible miracle.

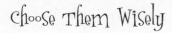

TS-S-S-S-S!

Let your burning desires
set the world on fire!

What do you want? Something for yourself? More happy, shiny friends? Better health? A new career? More money? More time? Or are your burning desires along the lines of helping others? Giving unceasingly? Lending a hand? Making a difference?

Think. Think. Think.

Ah-ha! I knew it. A true spiritual maestro, you want it all. Bravo! Now, please remember, if you really want to make a difference in the world, you will be most effective if first you are selfish.

Selfishness doesn't mean you don't love others; it simply means that you love yourself, that you honor your dreams and preferences, and that you finally understand you can make no one happy until you first get happy. And thus the pursuit of your happiness is the worthiest of all.

Besides, you're not here to save the world. You're here to save yourself from boredom and limitations. And as you soar, the world will become a better place.

YOUR PLACE IN TIME AND SPACE

The forest is hushed
with still fallen snow,
as the moon casts light
on the earth below.
There isn't a soul
on the planet tonight
not bathed in a love
from a faraway sight.
It's silent and still,
and throughout the land,
every living thing lies
in the palm of one hand.

Ever wonder how birds fly in such perfect formations? Or how a bear knows when to awaken in the spring? Or how bees and ants and other colonized critters always know what to do in relation to the thousands of others they live and work with? It's because they're all spiritually connected to one another and to their environment. But there's a better word than connected. They're all one. They operate as one, not because they're connected, but because they are one. And it doesn't stop there. They're all one with every other living thing—prey and predators, friends and enemies. How else could such an impossible balance be achieved in nature? The birds, the bears, the bees, the sky, the flowers, the trees, and, of course, people like you and me.

All the zillions of elements that physi-

cally sustain each unique and individual life, and the in-finite possibilities that allow for our unlimited growth and fulfillment play together like one colossal, multi-dimensional symphony that dwarfs the vast Universe known by our five senses.

God has many, many, many faces, and yours is one of them. One awareness with countless perspectives. This is where you fit in. And may you discover, enjoy, and revel in your oneness with it all.

Not a day has ever passed when every living soul wasn't bathed in a love from a distant site. And never has there ever been a single moment when we weren't all embraced and adored by the very same spirit that began the beating of our hearts.

And never has the sun risen on a day that was limited by the past nor has it set on a night without dreams. Neither has one minute of a life ever passed that didn't contain endless potentials for joy nor has there ever been a time when we weren't infinitely free to think as we please.

And the magic will never end, miracles will never cease, and it will never, ever get any better than this.

TREES TEACH

Visualize a planet
where all creatures are one
and happiness will flower
brighter than the sun!

Have you noticed it too? That trees teach? Here are seven of my favorite lessons:

1. Think first. Putting the right tree in the wrong place or the wrong tree in the right place could be as unfortunate as it might be costly.

2. It's always OK to change your mind. No matter how old your tree is, even if it's one hundred years old, it's never too late to relocate it if you really want to. Sure, there may be costs, even great costs, but often, even a simple little change can save years or a lifetime of floundering and unhappiness.

3. A little care goes a long way. It can even double their rate of growth.

4. Growth happens exponentially. Take, for example, a puny little stick of a tree that you might buy at your local nursery. With a little care, at the end of its first year, you'll have three more feet of tree. But by the end of its tenth year, your puny little stick will have at least one hundred major limbs, all of which will grow at least three feet, giving you three hundred more feet of tree in just that one year! The parallels in life are obvious. It works with everything you do. Life rewards effort exponentially.

5. Starting is the hardest part. Looking at any barren lot, it's virtually impossible to imagine that one day it might be wooded, until you start planting. And then, it's virtually impossible to see it any other way.

6. Diversify. If you planted only one little tree in your yard and year after year you cared and looked after it, you'd be fairly devastated if it were to succumb to lightning or a storm.

Whereas, if you planted several trees every year, the loss of any single tree, or even several, would be far less traumatic than losing your one and only. Diversify everything. It's easy.

7. Deal with it. You've never heard a tree complain or whine or feel sorry for itself. And you've never seen a tree run from its problems. Neither should we. This doesn't mean we have to welcome challenges into our lives, but we do have to deal with them in order to effect change.

And there's so much more! Trees bend, they never stop growing, they change with the seasons...

THE GREATEST CHALLENGE

Believe...

There's no greater challenge you will ever face than seeing through the illusions of time and space to the truths of being, to the understanding that nothing is ever lost, that there is only love, and that all things remain possible—including, and especially, those things that you wish for yourself.

And nothing will ever cause you greater pain or bring you more happiness than dealing with this challenge.

What I'm getting at is that truth is more quickly revealed when you follow your bliss, when you pursue your dreams, and when your life is about doing what you want to do. So see yourself in the picture, the picture of your dreams, because not only will you arrive but you'll be healed.

Challenges were part of the agreement you made with the Universe. And keeping the faith, believing, in spite of all evidence to the contrary, was one of the challenges you couldn't refuse. You're like that.

You are up to whatever challenges you now face, and the upside to this is really, really big.

Believe!

No Holds Barred

The fish in the sea
swim from shore to shore,
searching for meaning
on the ocean floor.
And we are the same
in time and space,
though what we need most
comes not from a place.

You've got questions. I know you've got questions. Should you stay or go? Should you quit or try harder? Should you search or let it come to you? Are you on the right path? Are you doing what you're "supposed" to be doing? Did you miss the boat? Is it too late?

Well, one thing's certain: There are no answers "out there." Look within. You are the living tissue of the Universe. Your intuition, your feelings, even your intellect are all hardwired to infinite wisdom. And no star, planet, number, card, friend, or confidant will ever get as close to your truth as you now are. You know it!

Whatever it is you want to know, ask yourself. And while you're at it, realize that there's no one answer to any question. There's no one path to abundance, health, and harmony. And it's never, ever, ever too late.

One more tip: To simplify virtually all of your questions, drop the shoulds and rephrase the question to, "What do I want to do?" Because what you want is what the Universe wants for you.

No holds barred.

UNSTOPPABLE

*It's you who decides
on your mission and fate.
For how else could you learn
of your gift to create?*

Really. If secret elements, lucky charms, or other "non-you" energies helped to craft your reality, how would you ever know what you were responsible for versus what was done by another? How would the credit be split? Mostly you or mostly them? What if something really bad happened? What if something really good happened? What if you wanted to initiate change in your life? Would you have to ask someone, would you have to get approval, would you have to wait?

Do you see? Any subjectivity in the matter of your destiny would entirely rob you of your creative sovereignty. No longer could it be said that "You shall reap as you sow," or "Believe, and all things are possible," or "Knock, and it shall be opened," because these would all be lies.

When the light goes on for the first time and you get this, it's kind of scary. You feel alone, even though you're not. But in time, it gets kind of exciting as the truth reminds you of how far you can reach. Better still, eventually it becomes impossible to see yourself as anything less than totally unlimited.

THE MAGNIFICENCE

A lot of time I wasted
wishing I could be
the opposite of everything
my mirror showed to me.
But then one day I realized
the only thing to do
was try to be a better me
and not another you.††

L ife is a "package deal." If today you were a bit wealthier, skinnier, smarter, or cuter than you already are, there might have been prices to pay in other areas of your life. Maybe you wouldn't be as insightful, spiritual, or compassionate as you are today. Or maybe you wouldn't laugh as much, help as much, or roll exactly the way you do now.

Get the picture? The events and circumstances, challenges and accomplishments that have shaped your life, that have left you wanting more of this and less of that have also honed

your finer senses and polished your character as nothing else could have.

This doesn't mean that there always needs to be these checks and balances, yins and yangs, or sacrifices for growth, because you've already paid your dues. Besides, there are no rules.

But realize they helped form the magnificence that you are today.

You are the package! Enjoy what you've earned. Bask in your radiance. And understand that your differences from others are also your advantages.

It's what you're made of! The Spirit of Life! Pure, 100 percent God "Stuff." Desire and energy born into time and space, burning and yearning to create and express, to dream and become, to live as you! Exactly as you wish to live.

The torch has been passed, and now, worlds wait to see what you will do.

E.T. Did It

You're never alone.

Let's just say, you're the mentor of a very, very special person—someone you love more than you even knew you could love. And let's just say that this very special person was about to embark on an extraordinary adventure—a multi-dimensional, twilight-zone kind of adventure with phenomenal opportunities for growth and fun, yet also one that could be fraught with fear and peril.

We'll say that you're comforted by the fact that you know they'll eventually return and be far more for having gone. But still, you're frightened too because you know it may be a long, long time before they'll see you again, even though you will always be as near to them as the air they breathe. And you're afraid that they'll get so carried away with the reality they're in that they may even forget their own identity and all that you've worked so hard on together.

At least, you think to yourself, where they go, I'll go, and what they feel, I'll feel, and always, whenever I'm called for—if I'm called for—I can make all the difference.

So what do you think your final words to your beloved protégé might be? No, better yet, what do you think your mentor might be trying to tell you? Right now? Mid-adventure?

"You're not alone. Let me help. Just ask."

P.S. "Phone home!"

THE ABCS OF MANIFESTATION

Always
do what you can,
with what you've got,
from where you are.

However, and this is really tricky but super important, don't expect that your efforts alone are what will make your dreams come true. Don't hinge the manifestation of your goals to what you do, but instead, understand that by doing all you can, you inspire the Universe to do all it can.

It's like this: You do *A*, the Universe does *B*, and you arrive at *C*. This is how everything works. *A* alone, however, will never get you to *C*. But it's the only way to get to *B*.

Now beware! If you forget about *B* and think that everything rides on *A*, you'll sweat the details, criticize yourself for not doing more and for not being better, and eventually convince yourself that you don't have "the right stuff," effectively decommissioning, firing, the Universe. Conversely, those who tend to think that everything rides on *B* often forget about *A* and go nowhere, while proclaiming that the Universe is alive with magic.

You must do all you can—not with the idea that what you do must be clever enough, fast enough, or sufficient enough to bring your dreams to life, but because your every effort will set invisible waves into motion, which will then summon all the elements to do your will.

Agh Ahem... It's me again... The Universe.

*Perspectives
summon
circumstances.*

I'm feeling kind of adventurous today. You?
Tell you what ... let's do away with some rules. Gravity for starters. Time too. Let's fly... and be young again. YOUNGER, I mean. Like kids.

Close your eyes and meet me over the very building you're now in ... hovering in space, looking down at its roof and off into the horizon that surrounds us. Imagine this as I go...

We're slowly gazing all around and soaking up the beauty that's everywhere. THEN, in a flash, everything's turned snowy white. Pure, radiant white ... above, below, and everywhere we look. NOTHING VISIBLE BUT WHITE... with one, micro-

scopic exception. In the distance, unimaginably far, far away...
we see what looks like a tiny, tiny, tiny speck... of GOLD.
Ummmmmm... gold is always good.

At first it appears that the gold is slowly, really slowly,
getting bigger ... but what's actually happening is that we are
getting closer to it. At first it seems we're moving slowly, but
actually, we're moving at the speed of light... then even faster,
it's just that the gold is so, so far away.

Ages pass, but the ride is awesome! Galaxies pass, but it's
sooooo exciting! Light years pass, but time stands still.

NOW... there's no more white. Just gold. Nowhere to go
because we're already there. And it turns out, this gold is so
much more than a color ... because you can HEAR it too...
kind of purring... and you can FEEL its luxurious warmth on

your skin, all over your body, and as you breath it, the aroma's like roses or plumeria or jasmine.

Most peculiar is that you sense IT'S ALIVE, supremely intelligent and acutely aware ... OF YOU. You know it knows, what you're thinking, what you're feeling, and it's as if your happiness is ALL that it cares about.

Not just alive, but responsive too, IMPRESSIONABLE, obliged even, to flood your physical senses ... with ALL that you can imagine ... like it's about to do.

Suddenly, the gold begins sparkling ... billions and billions of sparkles envelop you ... flashing, winking, shining ... and slowly, slowly, slowly ... it begins to fade away ... pixel for pixel, sparkle for sparkle, it begins manifesting itself into something ... even more spectacular, dazzling, and magical than what it was ... LO AND BEHOLD ...

Before your very eyes, right this very moment, the GOLD has transformed itself ... into ... TODAY ... and yet another day, in paradise. Wow. Welcome back.

By the way, the GOLD was me all along… so is today. And I love you with all of my heart.

Tallyho,
The Universe xxoo

P.S.—I had to turn the gravity back on … but you are still younger.

P.P.S.—Whenever you want a change of scenery, just summon the Gold.

HOW TO INSPIRE THE MAGIC

To be or not to be
depends on what you do.
For actions speak louder than words,
but to act is up to you.

Something magical happens when you act in line with your dreams, when you behave, at least once a day, as if your desire has already manifested. Actually, many things happen.

First, such an act actually suspends any hidden beliefs of yours that may have kept you from having whatever it is you want. This is good.

Second, you accomplish whatever the act was. Also good.

Third, you are physically revealing to the Universe that you do believe in your dream, the power, and forces unseen. Go you!

Fourth, you momentarily take your mind off of the lack or unfulfillment you've been experiencing, while your focus expands to include more thoughts that parallel such acts. Good.

Fifth, you feel the emotions that went along with your act, empowering the related thoughts to become things even faster. Also good.

Sixth, it's fun. Always good.

Seventh, you summon the Universe, inspiring its magic. You command it to pick up where you've left off, to act as you have acted, manipulating the people, events, and circumstances of your life in harmonious, mutually beneficial ways to make physical that which you have envisioned. Awesome.

It's so simple. Visualize once a day for five minutes. Perform one act of faith per day and you'll have the world in the palm of your hand.

TO DWELL OR NOT TO DWELL

Picture in your mind
all that you may be,
and with a little time
you will come to see
that in the game of life
your dreams will come alive
by thinking of the end result
as if it had arrived.

This is the Universe speaking. I think you've already noticed, but in case you haven't, all the same rules, laws, and principles that you've come to rely on in the past, like gravity, the speed of light, and "thoughts becoming things," will again apply in the future—especially the latter. You see, both gravity and light are relative. "Thoughts becoming things," however, is

absolute. It's the law. In fact, so long as you're thinking, you're it—the boss, the chief, top gun!

As you know, this is an incredible responsibility—huge! And it's filled with peril. All you have to do is dwell on your problems, your sorrows, your lacks, and your fears, and they will remain in your life. Similarly, this is an incredible opportunity—huge! And it's filled with promise. All you have to do is dwell on laughter and friendships, peace and harmony, love and abundance, and they will flood into your life.

Consequently, it is still highly recommended that you think good thoughts. After all, you have the choice, and you're still it!

BIG QUESTION

*Your angels are there
in your time of need,
not to question or judge,
but to give you a lead.
It may be a vision
or a voice you hear—
they just want to show you
that magic is near.
So pick yourself up
and go after your dream;
you could never have
a better home team!*

Angel asks, "Universe, what surprises you the most about humans?"

Universe replies, "Everything! Everything surprises me about humans! But what really takes my breath away is their endless capacity to rebound, adjust, and adapt, to hope and to dream no matter how rocky their road has been. They are the wind beneath my wings."

Ever feel like you're being watched? Admired? Loved and adored?

You are.

WAITING TO COME TRUE

A celebration of stars
dance into the night,
one for each dream
about to take flight.
And by dawn's early hour
they all have a plan
to burst into your life
as fast as they can.
But you've got to believe
that dreams really come true
if you want all the gifts
that are waiting for you!

Living the life of your dreams comes from aligning your beliefs with whatever it is that you want—not from virtues, not practice, not money, not patience, not connections, not tolerance, not religion, not meditation, not karma, not goodness, but beliefs. Then, when your beliefs are in line with your dreams, you can't help but think thoughts and begin moving in line with your dreams. You're helplessly drawn toward them through magically incited reality adjustments (coincidences)! And their manifestation becomes truly inevitable, as if they were meant to be.

Just believe.

THE PLAN

Most folks "there" are waiting for a sign
from folks "here" before they make a move,
take action, or commit.
Same "here."
Good thing we have eternity, huh?

But have you ever thought about what your plan is? Probably—probably way too much! But you're right to wonder, because there is a plan just for you that no other could ever hope to fulfill. And when you hear just how simple it is, you're liable to protest, as if you were an Olympic coach.

Your tailor-made plan is simply to be. To be yourself! To make your decisions, to follow your heart, to experience time and space as only you can with your gifted insights, dispositions, and desires. No one else will ever be able to do that. Not from where you've come from.

Wait! There's more! Something's shaking! Quake! Rumble! Lightning bolt! The sky parts...

"This is the Universe. And you? You are my only chance to be you. All that you are and hope to become is what we've dreamed together. And with each journey you take, you are my eyes, ears, and heart. You give me tears to cry and laughter to

roar. I may be the rain in the spring and the leaves in the fall, but without your unique perceptions, so much would be lost forever.

"And there's more! For the countless lives you touch, there I am, too—changed.

"You being you is unimaginably important. So, maybe, for now, don't even try.

"Just be."

Sky closes back up.

IT'S NOT AS IF

To be all you can be,
to give all you can give,
to love all you can love,
and to live all you can live—
just ask.

After all, it's not as if you haven't already done enough; your presence here hasn't changed everything; eternity doesn't now lie before you; new friends, magic, and laughter don't await; you aren't now bathed in showers of unconditional love, held in the palm of another without a million reasons to give thanks!

Besides, at this very minute the Universe is peering over your shoulder, reading these words with you, still at your beck and call, and ready to start anew with wherever today has found you.

You're not alone.

Heck, what more could you ask for?

Saddle up!

Don't go it alone! The entire Universe will conspire in your favor if you let it. Remember, you've been given dominion over all things, and it's not just because you're so smart and good looking. It's because all the elements will gladly do your will if and when you ask. Asking opens the door. It points the way. It's the crystallization of desire and will into the form of your thoughts. And you know what happens from there— they become the things, people, circumstances, and events of your life.

The power and the glory are yours. Just ask!

A-PLUS!

Do not look down upon another,
or judge the days they keep.
Mere thoughts can wound like daggers
that cause the sky to weep.
Each one of us is special,
with a mystery all our own.
And left to walk our own path,
we'll sooner make it home.

Not that you would because you well know that everyone is doing their best. But are you so kind with yourself?

Well, "sometimes" doesn't cut it.

Your life is not a test that will be graded based upon what you do or don't do, what you say or don't say, or even upon what you think and believe!

That you are simply here is acing it, partaking in an adventure where it can seem that you're less than you really are—powerless, alone, and limited—instead of invincible, loved, and infinite.

You have done your best. And it's been more than enough. The truth always wins out. And so will you!

BE TRUE TO YOU

Be true to yourself
in the games that you play,
or it could be your dreams
that you one day betray.

What do you want? Have you made it a priority? You can't give all that you have to give, to yourself and the world, unless you are first true to yourself. Sound selfish? Good! Selfishness doesn't mean you don't care for others, and it doesn't mean you don't lend a hand where needed. It does mean that you understand that your fulfillment, happiness, and laughter count—big time! It means realizing that your greatest responsibility as a human is not to save the world but to save yourself, because no one else can or will. And it means honoring your own passions, instincts, and desires so that you can always hear the call of your dreams and respond.

Then, as your dreams begin coming true, others will benefit, even people you don't know. Your life begins getting easier. Your vibrations are raised. You begin living with a newfound lightness, projecting an aura that shines onto the darkened paths of others. And the world does, in the end, become a much better place, thanks to the example you've become.

The Ultimate Power Tool

Money is power;
it puts shoes on your feet.
But that power is limited
by the time that you keep.
You can charge by the hour
or the seeds that you sow.
It makes little difference
if you really want to know.
Because the mark
of achievement
for your time in the sun
is the love that you shared
before your life was done.

Your life touches so many other lives, it's impossible to calculate. And then, those lives touch so many and those lives touch so many and those lives touch so many, and on and on and on.

The same is true of the love you share, whether it's raising a child, helping a stranger, or caring for an animal. The good just goes and goes and goes. And it grows and grows and grows.

If you had any idea, just the faintest idea, of how powerful a kind act is, of just how far it can reach into the lives and consciousness of the planet, today and far off into the future, you'd probably freak! Just lose it! Fall over, get back up, and fall over again! But you'd recover. And then you'd beam, like the sun, so happy for all the kindness you've already shared. And then you'd cry, just a bit, for the opportunities that were missed. But then you'd beam like the sun again because it's never too late to touch someone else and make a huge difference. And then, little else would matter.

Do you have to feel your heart beating to know that it does? Hardly, but it makes all the difference for you and others, because in a thousand little ways, at a thousand points throughout each day, with your every smile, wave, and nod, the world gets a little bit better.

NICE JEANS

*The mightiest works
start with the smallest steps.*

Okay, okay, okay, so you don't really have to "do all you can, with what you've got, from where you are" to rock the world. Nope. You can just think it rocked and it will be rocked. The same is true for walking on water and manifesting gold coins from your blue jeans. You have the technology.

Oh. Still reading? Hmmmm, odd. I mean if you can manifest gold coins from your blue jeans...

Ah-ha. Other beliefs. I see. Invisible, limiting beliefs that you've been programmed with by a base, primitive society that says you're a weak, mortal, biological accident, lucky to have risen from the seas. Darn.

OK. How about this:

From here on out, you just do all that you can, with what you've got, from where you are. Then, the Universe gets to have all the fun, pouncing on every chance you get, seamlessly weaving miracle upon miracle together—not so obviously that people might want to burn you—playing and ricocheting off those pesky, Neanderthal beliefs, and the next thing you know, you'll be past them. They'll evaporate since you will have trumped them with your manifestations, and you'll be back to doing things without doing things.

The more you do, the easier it is to navigate around limits you may not have even known were yours. And best of all, once we blow past them, they teeter over—whether or not you ever became aware of them.

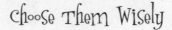

EERIE

The call of a whale
to those out of reach
echoes a secret
they long to teach:
That material things
quickly sink out of view,
but time shared with a friend
is forever with you.

It makes such a difference. It can mean so much. It takes so little to smile, to listen intently, to offer help before asked. And always, you are watched—seen by the unseen. Your deeds are never forgotten, never for naught. Your demonstrations are recorded as "proof" that you believe you live in a caring world; and so, such a world is manifested for you, proof that you believe there's always time for kindness. And this world will become even kinder to you, proof that you believe you live in a giving world. And this world will give greatly to you but never in like measures. For when you give as mightily as you can, an infinite Universe gives to you as mightily as it can. And the good is amplified and a cycle begun.

INFINITE POSSIBILITIES

Walk in the green forest of silence,
swim in the blue ocean of joy,
dance in the golden light of love,
and laugh in the raging river of life.†

Everything matters—everything. Every single word you speak, every single deed you perform, and every single thought you think is recorded and reverberates throughout eternity. Yet nothing is so important that it can take away from the infinite possibilities that will always lie before you—possibilities that carry the potential for love, joy, and laughter such as you've never known. No matter where you've been, no matter where you are, the best is yet to come.

Everything matters! Not because time is fleeting but because your dreams are waiting.

BUST A MOVE

I'm history in the making,
and I want the world to know:
Whether you think I'm a fool or a hero,
you're in for one heck of a show!

Why is it that those things which are free, abundant, and commonplace, like time, family, and friends, are so easily taken for granted until we have to go without? Or perhaps until we allow them to slip through our fingers?

Hmmm...

Every hour, week, and year that passes brings that great curtain call a little bit closer. And between now and then, every single day is an opportunity, a second chance to follow your heart, to appreciate what already is, and to make a difference. Use it! Use it all—every precious second—to dare, to reach, and to try. Not because there won't be other chances—there will be—but because the unimaginable glory that awaits you is magnified by your every effort.

READY, AIM, FIRE!

If all the "want"
were squelched in me,
there'd be no march
through eternity.

Without a port, the ship will stay at sea. Without a target, the arrow hits the ground. Without a destination, the journey's incomplete. And without desire, a soul is half alive.

Fellow adventurer, let your heart choose your targets in time and space. Fill yourself with expectation and revel in the awareness that your desires are meant to be.

GET UP, GET OUT

Be bold and go forth
like it was meant to be.
Your dreams are the gifts
that will set you free.

Nothing throws the gears of the Universe into motion quicker than your actions. So when it comes to living the life of your dreams, begin simply by doing what you can.

When you do what you can, the Universe responds in kind, doing what it can with an infinitely greater and farther reach than your own. Suddenly, supernatural chain reactions are triggered that would never have otherwise been triggered. New avenues become available, and new vistas and vantages become apparent. Work is done behind the scenes, new characters are introduced, and the script is completely rewritten. Expectations are exceeded, sights are raised, and forces unseen propel you onwards, all because you simply did what you could.

Don't wait for your every duck to be lined up. Do what you can this week!

FORE!

Think it, talk it,
live it, show it.
Whatever you want,
let the Universe know it.

Invoke the law! Give it to the Universe, and the Universe has to give it back to you.

What happens when someone hits a ball into the air? Well, about halfway through its arc it falls back to earth, right? Why? It's the law. It has to. Now, does it matter who was putting? Does it matter how old they are, how smart they are, how "good" they are, how faithful, forgiven, religious, or spiritual they are? Does it matter how popular they are, how good looking they are, how influential they are, how enlightened they are? Does anything matter once the ball has been hit? Heck, no!

And neither does anything matter once you invoke the laws of manifestation and the principle of thoughts becoming things, no matter what your thoughts may be—be they visualizations or daydreams.

You've been blessed with dominion over all things. Period. And this blessing is not contingent upon anything other than you, just as you now are, exercising the principles that are already at play in the Universe.

Fore!

THINK 'EM

What once was a dream
has now come to pass,
as the stone and the clay
were first ether and gas.
And so it has been
in time and in space,
where all of your thoughts
yearn for their place.
They are here on earth
on the day they're conceived
and brought to life
once you really believe.

Hardly wishful thinking! It's the cold hard truth! Your thoughts are everything! And when you believe in the likelihood of their manifestation, and you keenly desire, or fear, their appearance in your life, you are helplessly and unavoidably drawn to think 'em, think 'em, and think 'em. Then, as your life unfolds, you'll be silently drawn into accidents, coincidences, and circumstances that enable your thoughts to become the things and events of your life.

Do you see the formula? It's like a game. Can you imagine the possibilities?

First, conceive. Decide on what you really, really want. Be crystal clear. Second, believe. Work through your beliefs to understand its feasibility. Remember, you live in a world of illusions with a Universe conspiring on your behalf, possessing unfailing principles. Your will must be done. Third, achieve. Be true to yourself and follow your heart.

Return to go. Repeat steps one through three. Become an example. Do it again. Light the way for others. Do it again. Live the life of your dreams.

Do this! Do it today! Sneak out a pencil and a Post-it note and, at a minimum, write down one goal to think about. It really, really works!!!

UNBROKEN

Unlimited, mysterious,
powerful, sublime
are the least that you are
in space and time.

The very least that you are! You ride upon a wave set into motion by a Being of Light who illuminated space and time with love, light, and magic so that you might carry the baton and take this adventure to an even higher level.

With your priceless perspectives, compassion, and insights, your job now, your responsibility to All That Is, is simply to honor yourself. Accept, approve, and confirm yourself. Love, respect, and obey yourself. Believe in your dreams, forgive your faults, and focus on the beauty, the endless beauty.

Then, the promise will be kept, the ring unbroken, and the burden for those who are to follow in your footsteps lightened.

Now, you are the light!

Everything Matters!

Some presents are big;
some presents are small.
But those from the heart
are the best ones of all.

Just being you packs more punch than you've ever realized. You are one of a kind. Not one in a billion or zillion, but a one and only.

The difference you make, with every word you speak and every action you take, changes the course of history. If you only knew how everything matters—everything you say, everything you do, and everything you think. It all goes out, and it all comes back—every wave, call, and smile, every fantasy, daydream, and wish. And to those in your circle? They're all touched. They're all affected. They're all changed. Your presence in any crowd is a gift to one and all. You wield more power than you've ever known. But now that you do know, enjoy the giving.

HOW?

Let there be magic
in all that you do.
It's part of the promise
that life made to you.

Perhaps the number one stumbling block between people and their dreams, and the number one limiting belief that shoots dreams out of the sky is that once you finally decide on what you really, really want, you then begin the regretful process of trying to figure out exactly how you're going to get there.

Not that you shouldn't have a game plan for doing what you can, because you should, but we erroneously think we must then orchestrate every tiny step along the way, finagle every twist of fate, and force every "lucky" break.

Don't go there! Don't even try! It's impossible! Leave the

hows to the Universe. We're little more than lumps of breathing clay. We can't even walk and talk without the unending miracles that support us. Yet, we want to insist that when it comes to achieving our loftiest ambitions, our physical selves do all the work!

Let there be magic in all that you do. Count on it! Expect it! It's there anyway, breathing for you, thinking for you, walking and talking for you. So why not use it when it comes to dream manifestation?

Besides, could it be easier?

HOW STARS ARE ALIGNED

It takes so little to do so much ...
Yet what little it takes is absolutely mandatory.

If you just whistle every now and then; skip every thousandth step or so; toss the odd stone across the odd pond; go dancing on the occasional blue moon, if only alone in the dark; dress up sometimes, even with nowhere to go ... Simply stirring up some little bit of hope—no matter how silly or disconnected your actions seem to be with the rest of the world—magic flashes in the unseen, friends are summoned, connections are timed, stars are aligned, opportunities are crystallized, and serendipities are calculated, creating possibilities for new realities that cannot now even be imagined from where you presently stand.

And you thought "buy low, sell high" was sage advice.

Shazaam!

NICE BLOOM

*If every flower
tried to look like another,
they'd forget that they're special
and unlike any other.*

How is it that you see least what those closest to you see most—that you're rare and beautiful, strong and able, accomplished and successful? It shouldn't be like this. It's time you saw what the rest of us see, that you're already enough as is, that you deserve to see your dreams manifest, and that you've already bloomed into the kind of person you dreamed you'd one day become.

OK? Beginning to see?

It just takes a little practice.

DID YOU HEAR THAT?

The miracle of the ocean
is the same in you and me:
Whatever it is we think on
will soon come to be.
Imagination is the force
that turns our lives around.
Like the currents underwater,
it moves without a sound.
Believe that you can do it
and know you have the powers.
Then, all good things will come to pass
as the waves unfold the hours.

Here's a tip to help you put the above to use: Did you notice the line that says "it moves without a sound"? Well, you already know that, right? Just as you know that it moves just out of sight. And you know that you cannot smell it, taste it, or feel it either, right? Right!

So keep in mind that just because you can't see your dreams coming true doesn't mean they aren't. Remember this during lulls in your week, month, or year. Just because you are not consciously aware of the wonderful "accidents" and serendipitous "coincidences" that you're about to experience doesn't mean that these ducks aren't now being lined up! Even as you read this, in the cosmos that now surrounds you and holds you in the palm of its hand, things are happening in your favor.

In short, don't judge your progress by what your physical senses now show you!

PRESENTS FOR YOU!

Take your time
and worry no more;
rushing around
won't settle the score.
The voice within
knows what you should do,
just listen to it
and follow through.

You are blessed with "gifts from Heaven." And these gifts are your instincts, hunches, impulses, and intuitions. These bursts of insight illuminate truths about your reality, yourself, and the life you're in the middle of creating. They're available to you as if through your own private window to the divine, and they often appear when you least expect them. But by training yourself to seek them out, the wisdom they offer can be added to your own arsenal of truth.

Keep this window open, practice gazing through it, and begin appreciating its priceless view. Use your gifts to find meaning, get direction, and to take steps toward making your dreams come true.

Whenever you have a question or a big decision to make, close your eyes and ask for help. Then see yourself exercising your different options and notice which feels better and which offers resistance.

Recognized or not, used or not, you do have a sixth sense, and best of all, it's there to help you have fun and be happy!

HOW TO LIVE LONG

Be free, live now.
Give hope, show how.
Share love, take care.
Stand tall, play fair.
Know right from wrong.
Be happy, live long.

Some very simple rules for a very simple game: the game of life. And whether you realize it or not, you're already a winner. You were born a winner.

No matter where you find yourself today, no matter how you may have tripped and stumbled in the past, you're still a winner. You've always done your best, and though you may now wish you had done a few things differently, at least your course has brought you to today. And the best thing about today is that now you're free to paint the present, and tomorrow, any color you like.

You're free to think the thoughts that will next become the things and events of your life. And you stand before the rest of your life with the greatest of allies: a loving, caring, invisible Universe that is now conspiring tirelessly in your favor; a living

Universe that gets out of bed when you do, drives to work with you, and even now sits beside you.

If it's not already clear, it will be before long. The reason you are where you are today with the wisdom, love, and understandings that your life has instilled in you is so that you can fully enjoy and appreciate the splendors that are now being laid out before you.

You go!

Hey, did you realize that the Universe doesn't conspire on your behalf based upon need? That it doesn't conspire on your behalf once you're deserving? That it doesn't care what you did or didn't do in the past? That it doesn't care what you will or won't do today? And that it doesn't care if you ask, it doesn't care if you pray, it doesn't even care what you think?

Nothing can turn it off! It's always conspiring!

Which means right now, between these very words, it's there conspiring to carry you through today, this week, and eternity on clouds of silver, wings of gold, and chariots of fire.

FEEL IT. PROVE IT.

I am a thought;
I make dreams come true
but that's just the half
of what thoughts can do.
Please use great care
when you choose what you think,
because whatever it is
may appear in a blink.
That's what we do
in time and in space,
as soon as we're thought,
we look for our place.
For better or worse,
to win or to lose,
the thing to remember
is that you get to choose!

What a gift! What power! You get to choose what you think and, thus, how your life will unfold.

Seems too easy, doesn't it? That's because we're so accustomed to letting the things and events of time and space tell us what and how to think, completely oblivious to the fact that the things of time and space sprang from our earlier thoughts.

It's time you break this cycle! Begin seeing yourself as the starting point of your experiences not the life that now surrounds you. And start imagining yourself living the life of your dreams—visualize!—without regard to your old thoughts and their present manifestations. Hold on tight to these new thoughts and don't let the world shake them from your grasp. Then, as your new thoughts begin taking hold and bearing fruit, remember how you did it so that you can begin proving to yourself, once and for all, that this principle of thoughts becoming things is absolute, immutable, and the greatest gift you've ever been given!

This ain't Kansas, Toto, and this ain't any ordinary adventure. Here, the truth is stranger than fiction. And it will set you free from boredom, routine, and stagnation. The truth I'm speaking of is that you are an unlimited Being of Light equipped with all you need to have all you want. And what's required of you is simply that you begin acting like an unlimited Being of Light. Start. You don't have to be perfect—just do your best. If you fall, get up. One day at a time.

Be the spark that lights the fire of change in your heart and in the hearts of all those fortunate enough to cross your path. Break a habit, change a pattern, pitch the kid gloves. And by your actions, you'll proclaim to the entire Universe that nothing will ever be the same. So be it. Hallelujah!

NEXT!

Our paths have crossed
on our way back home,
making small the price
of times spent alone.

Allow your joys to ebb and flow. Don't define spells of uncertainty, loneliness, or unhappiness as the way things are, because they are not the way things are. You always have something to look forward to, whether you know what that something is or not. And best of all, it's not just a "something;" it's the best of times and the best of friends. New adventures, experiences, and circumstances lie just around the corner, and they need only your expectation to transpire and manifest.

Laughter such as you've never known, peace such as you have never experienced, love such as you've never felt, and fun!

These aren't just for the fortunate, the blessed, or the holy; they're your inalienable birthrights. No matter what you think you deserve, you do deserve these—always have, always will. Stake your claim, look ahead, and know of the happiness that awaits you.

SOAR

I am the bird in flight
and the sky it seeks.
I am the sun at dawn
rising over the peaks.
I am the voice you hear
when the clouds turn gray
and the hand you hold
when you've lost your way.
And though you forget me
from time to time,
even now I am with you
as you read this rhyme.

Peering through your eyes, feeling through your heart, thinking all your thoughts, and I am so pleased—so pleased that you are exactly who you are. That is enough. You are magnificent! Give it to yourself today. Today, just know that you're divine. Know that your so-called flaws pale in comparison to your greatness. You may have lost your wings, but even now you soar, and I am the wind beneath you.

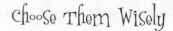
FRUITS OF LIFE

The weather may storm
and the bow may break
on the quest for treasure
we all must make.
But when the chest is found
and the gold revealed,
the secret of life
remains concealed.
Because that which we seek
lies not in the sand
but in the hearts and souls
of every woman and man.

And that which we seek is right and noble and good. Even if all you're really after are bags of money and pots of gold. It's all good, because the destination is illusive, always changing, and completely irrelevant. The destination is what inspires the journey, and it's the journey that's laden with treasure, such as victories and failures, happiness and gloom, romance and heartbreak. These are the fruits of life, because one day, when they're all tallied up together, they'll remind you of how invincible you were, how powerful you are, and how rich you've become—thanks to the dreams, material or otherwise, that inspired you.

You can't go wrong nor have you.

LEAD THE WAY

Warning!
Thoughts (still) become things—
choose them wisely.

There may be a war on the horizon, there may be more unemployment, and the stock market may slide. But what the heck does any of this have to do with you? Absolutely nothing, because the inviolate principle of thoughts becoming things is completely blind to the goings on of the world in general while totally mindful of you and subservient to the thoughts that you choose to think.

Have you thought of taking a vacation in the days, weeks, and months ahead? Did you want to find a new job, career, or special someone? Were you expecting your life to take off? Then all hands on deck, because you remain at the helm of your ship, terrorists or no terrorists, war or no war. Life remains ripe and abundant for those who think in those terms. For every door that's just closed, twelve more opened, just for you. There is a way! The physical route you take may be altered, but you will get, you have to get, what you choose to focus on in the precious, formative days to come.

Don't compromise. Prepare for the time of your life!

THE GREATEST SECRET

*Like the sound of waves
crashing onto the beach
or the call of a gull
to those out of reach,
life's wonders are hidden
in the world around you,
and each time you find one
you're given a clue
to the magic of life
and the mystery it keeps,
where never a dream
lies outside of your reach.*

Of all life's wonders, your presence here is the greatest, though sadly, for the moment, you can't comprehend your own magnificence and importance.

Were it not for you and your life, as you've lived it thus far, nothing on this planet would be quite the same as it is today. This is also more truthful than you can now comprehend.

You're not one of six billion; you're one-of-a-kind, extraordinary, rare, and precious with a reach and power that would boggle the mind. Your thoughts touch us all, your kindness heals, and your compassion lifts spirits. The good you've done will carry on indefinitely. If you only knew of the difference you've already made. If you only knew of the difference you're now making. If you only knew that you only ever have to be you.

Let the magic of life remind you of your own miracle.

Traits of the Immortal

By the time you're really rolling,
it will be in a direction
you cannot now even imagine,
so please, for the time being, just roll.

There comes a day in the evolution of every spiritual being when their inner yearnings, struggles, and frustrations bring them to a truth that could not have otherwise been achieved along the sometimes dark road that leads to enlightenment. And so, dearly beloved, I now come with such a truth, knowing it may temporarily hurt eyes that have been shut too long. Reaching this milestone was inevitable, for the light that will dawn hereafter is not only what you have summoned but what all have summoned. And with your blessing and recognition, this light will bathe all who follow in your footsteps, and the burden they bear shall be lessened.

If it's not yet obvious to you, the real reason for time and space … is you. A more perfect child of the Universe has never existed. Until now, only stories cloaked in myth and mystery could hint at your sublime heritage and divine destiny. You are life's prayer of becoming and its answer—the first light at the dawn of eternity, drawn from the ether so that the Universe might know its depths, discover its heights, and revel in seas of emotion. You are a pioneer into illusion, an adventurer into the unknown, a lifter of veils—courageous, heroic, and exalted by countless souls in the unseen.

To give beyond reason; to care beyond hope; to love without limit; to reach, stretch, and dream in spite of fear: These are the hallmarks of divinity—traits of the immortal—your badges of honor, and the only way home.

SHINE OUT LOUD!

When U
R U
U R
Unique.†

D o you have any idea who you really are? Do you have any idea of your effect on others? Do you know what it's like to be touched by you? To be held in your glance? To be smiled at by you? Do you even know what it's like to brush up alongside of you in the streets? To see you from a distance? Up close? Do you know what it's like to see you approaching? Do you know what it's like to watch you walk away? Do you know what it does for someone when they realize that you've been thinking of them?

No, you don't. Kind of sad. Your insights, beauty, strength, courage, and humility change lives everyday and you don't even

know it. It's especially sad because those you touch think you do, so they might not remind you.

Since you don't know it and since others may not tell you, let me.

You are a light in the darkness—a bringer of the dawn. Your touch heals, your gaze inspires, and your smile is like cool water to parched lips. The sight of you stirs one's spirit, and your departure is always too soon. Your profoundly unique journey has been one-of-a-kind, and it has yielded compassion and insights as rare as yourself—gifts that sparkle like a diamond in the sun.

You are a pillar, an icon, and a champion to those who know you and to those who wish they did. Your effect on the world today, as you are, where you are, is awesome.

Shine your light because, while your significance may sometimes escape you, it changes others forever.

TOTALLY CRAZY

The deep blue sea
spoke to me;
it was holding back
a mystery.
A dolphin took me by the hand;
it wanted me to understand
that in this life
there's more to behold
than bags of money and pots of gold.
Believe in yourself
and you will see
how happy and free
you were meant to be.‡

And the totally crazy thing is that when you do believe in yourself, things, material things, maybe even bags of money and pots of gold, begin showing up in your life, almost inexplicably.

But actually, it's all quite explicable.

You see, when you truly believe in yourself, you stop living in the past and your regrets and sorrows disappear. You stop worrying about the future and your doubts and fears fall away. You stop focusing on what you're not and begin seeing all that you already are.

Then, with your mind as calm as a glassy sea, you effortlessly think thoughts of gratitude for the present and for your dreams tomorrow. These thoughts will then do what all thoughts must do: strive to become the things and events of your life. But this time around, now that you believe in yourself, they'll have much less competition.

THE LAST DANCE

*It's not the score
or how often you win,
but that you face the fears
that lurk within.*

Because never have you ever had anything to fear. Here's a trick: Whenever you hear the tigers you most dread prowling through the jungles of your mind, close your eyes and let them loose.

Imagine the beasts having their way. Yes, visualize the worst. Imagine the agony. Feel the suffering. Hear the screams. Do this.

Of course, thoughts do become things. But this is all the more reason to hurry up about it, lest these tigers stalk you day in and day out, week in and week out, year in and year out, as you fight to resist, avert, and outmaneuver their cunning rather than face them for a few minutes out in the open.

And if on the outside chance you remain conscious, still breathing, perhaps still sitting in the very same chair, you'll see that these feline foes had about as much power as if they were painted on paper. And if you don't feel like laughing out loud, at least you'll have freed your mind for some good thoughts.

It really works. But you have to set them free and look them right in the eye.

After all, you're bigger than the demons you've imagined. You'll outlast them. You always have.

And you remain in a Universe that all along has been preparing to shower you with more gifts than there's room to receive.

You'll get the last word. You'll have the last dance. But first there's more painting to do.

PILLOW FIGHT!

Sometimes, you laugh so hard
it starts a hurricane in the heavens.
Sometimes, you grin so wide
it causes earthquakes on distant planets.

As a child, it seems like the entire world is there for you, and you rush to drink from its every cup, sometimes wondering to yourself how anything could ever be more fun. You catch raindrops on your tongue, explore and build forts, roll around and dig at the beach. You spend lazy afternoons just lying on the grass, looking for shapes in the clouds or sticking gummy bears up your nose.

Then, as you grow older, if you're observant, you realize much of what you enjoy was made possible by the contributions of those who came before you, and you're taken aback, disappointed even, because with maturity you can now see cracks in the façades, imperfections in the details, and ten thousand ways it could have all been done better.

At which point, folks typically choose one of two paths: spend a lifetime lamenting how far from perfect things are or, to one degree or another, roll up their sleeves and pitch in.

And should they choose the latter with gusto, they will come to know, to the core of their sacred being, that the differences they might make in the world cannot be made by another. And then they will discover the answer to their often-wondered childhood question, discovering that the most fun one can have in time and space comes from making such a difference and that the joy derived from serving is ten thousand times that of being served.

This doesn't mean life becomes all work and no play. It just means work becomes play, no matter what you do, and play becomes ecstasy.

YOUR TURN

Live, laugh, love, and have fun!
Just a moment more
and your turn will be done.

Heavy but true. Right here and now, it's your turn. What greater motivation could exist than knowing it won't always be your turn? What error could you make or how badly could you fail that its occurrence could compare to the loss of not trying and never knowing?

Of course, you are eternal, and it's quite possible that the gift you've set out to experience will lie in your silence and calm. But if it's fear that's holding you back from being true to yourself, then maybe it's time to counter it with the understanding that for now you can do something about it.

Life here, in time and space, is where we learn our lessons, experiment, and grow. These are the reasons we're here— to find out who and what we really are. You're not here to be Superman, Superwoman, or superhuman. You're here to be you. And by being you, you'll learn your lessons, make your mark, and be happily on your way to the next great adventure.

Mistakes, failure, and fear are par for the course. They help make it a course. They're part of the adventure, and they're OK. Work with them, deal with them, face them, and before long, you'll laugh at them. And you'll be glad for the lessons they taught.

AFTERWORD

I t's now been eight years since I wrote the majority of this book, during a great transition in my life. It was a scary time and one fraught with timidity and self-doubt.

It took me three weeks to get up the courage to include a little passage of my insights with each "Monday Morning Motivator." I remember wanting to do it, but then hearing a chorus of objections in my mind of how readers might reply: "Who cares, Mike?" "How conceited to think you might have something to offer that others will find enriching!" "You're only offering common sense stuff, nothing that couldn't be gleaned from hundreds of books!" Yet my subscribers surprised me by asking for more. It turned out the chorus wasn't from my readers but from my own fears and insecurities. Lesson learned: If you want to do something, do it! Follow your heart! Don't worry about what others may think!

I also learned that by starting a task, by committing to it, it's as if the entire Universe jumps on your bandwagon. Many a morning I sat in front of a blank computer screen, absolutely clueless as to what I might write. Had I waited for inspiration, I'm quite sure it never would have come. But by literally forcing myself to write, sometimes writing anything that came to mind, this physical step into the unknown somehow summoned the resources, thoughts, and insights that I would end up sharing.

Of course, there were times when I wrote and wrote, and I never felt too pleased with the result, but then I learned something else: to insist. I would insist that I continue writing until I liked what I wrote, even though this

insistence often turned a one-hour project into a four- or six-hour project. That part, honestly, I hated; waiting until I was happy, never knowing exactly when such a goal would be achieved. It was torturous. Nevertheless, it was through insistence, not acceptance or praise of myself for trying, that I persevered and always achieved what I was after.

Perhaps the greatest lessons from my journey came from actually applying what I was teaching to my life, witnessing how my free Monday mailings evolved to take me down paths I never could have imagined and eventually into a career as a teacher on the nature of reality, which now has me leading a truly fairytale existence. Had I worried about or tried to manipulate the hows of my life, getting really logical or practical, it wouldn't have happened in a million years. I also learned that by following my heart in spite of my timidity and by taking action in spite of its seeming futility, my future successes were exponentially greater than my efforts. And I discovered that by refusing to view setbacks as failures, by never ceasing with my baby steps, sometimes while unable to even discern the path I was on, I gave the Universe the ability to connect the dots and get in on the game, crafting a life that has already exceeded my wildest dreams.

And now, I believe, it's your turn.